EXPLORING
MATHEMATICS
THROUGH
HISTORY

CAMBRIDGE
UNIVERSITY PRESS

Published by the Press Syndicate of the University of Cambridge
The Pitt Building, Trumpington Street, Cambridge CB2 1RP
40 West 20th Street, New York, NY 10011-4211, USA
10 Stamford Road, Oakleigh, Melbourne 3166, Australia

First published 1995

Produced by Gecko Ltd, Bicester, Oxon

Printed in Great Britain by Scotprint Ltd, Musselburgh, Scotland

A catalogue record for this book is available from the British Library

Library of Congress cataloguing in publication data

Eagle, M. Ruth.
Exploring mathematics through history/M. Ruth Eagle.
        p.   cm.
Includes bibliographical references (pp. 104–105) and index.
ISBN 0 521 45626 6 (paperback)
1. Mathematics – History.   I. Title.
QA21.E24   1995
510'.71'2 – dc20   95–13797   CIP

ISBN 0 521 45626 6 paperback

Contents

Acknowledgements

Too many people have contributed to this book for me to name them all, but this is my opportunity to thank everyone most heartily. Students, pupils and teachers have helped, perhaps without knowing it. I value the ideas and suggestions which have come from many quarters. Rick and Peter have been particularly generous with their time and advice. Joe was wonderfully willing and prompt when I needed a translation. Others have helped with vital pieces of information and technical assistance. I should particularly like to thank all the library and museum staff who have responded so cordially to my enquiries.

Piecing together suitable material is a fascinating task, but the effort of compiling a book sprang from Dick's encouragement to get started. It has only proceeded along with the heartening support of friends and colleagues along the way. My pre-occupation whilst writing it may have been a trial, but foremost with interest and patience has been Robert, and to him I dedicate this work.   *M. Ruth Eagle*

The author and publisher would like to acknowledge the following as sources of quotations. Fuller details of references are given in the bibliography.

Key: *t* = top, *b* = bottom, *c* = centre, *l* = left, *r* = right
Numbers in **bold** refer to resource sheets. **F** = folio

M.G. Agnesi 94*c*, **15.3**, **15.4** (adapted from *Institutioni Analitiche*, tr. J. Colson)

J. Babington **8.2***t*, **8.3***lt*, **8.4***lt* (*A Short Treatise of Geometrie*)

G. Cardano 45 (*The Book of My Life*, tr. J. Stoner, Dent 1931); **F5***lc*, *lb* (adapted from *The Great Art: or The Rules of Algebra*, tr. T.R. Witmer, MIT Press 1968)

F.N. David 84*lc*, **13.1**, **13.2** , **13.3** (abridged from *Games, Gods and Gambling*, Griffin 1962)

J. Dee 65*lc* (Preface to *The Elements of Geometry of Euclid*, H. Billingsley, 1570)

O.L. Dick **5.4***r*, 54*lt* (*Aubrey's Brief Lives*, Penguin 1987)

Edinburgh Review 75*rt* (1808, Vol. 11, pp. 282–3)

R.J. Gillings **7.3***rb* (*Mathematics in the Time of the Pharoahs*, Dover 1982)

T.L. Heath 32*lt*, 32*rc*, 32–33 (*The Works of Archimedes*, 1897)

L.C. Jain 34*lb* (*Exact Sciences from Jaina Sources*, Vol. 2, Rajastha Jaipur 1982)

G.G. Joseph 31*rt* (*The Crest of the Peacock: Non-European Roots of Mathematics*, I.B. Tauris 1991)

The Ladies' Diary **12.1**, **12.2**, **12.3** (1707–13)

W. Leybourn **9.5***lb*, **11.1**, **11.2**, **11.3** (*Cursus Mathematicus: Mathematical Sciences in Nine Books*)

A. Maurel **15.1***lb–r* (*The Romance of Mme du Chatelet and Voltaire*, tr. W. Mostyn, Hutchinson, reproduced by kind permission of the publishers)

K. Menninger 31*lc* (*Number Words and Number Symbols*, tr. P. Broneer, MIT Press 1969)

A. de Moivre 85*rt*, **13.4** (*The Doctrine of Chances*)

W. Mudge and I. Dalby **11.4**, **11.6** (*An Account of the Operations Carried on for Accomplishing a Trigonometrical Survey of England and Wales*, Vol. 1, 1799)

J. Needham **F2***tr* (*Science and Civilisation in China*, Cambridge University Press 1959)

I. Newton 90*rc*, **14.1***b* (*The Mathematical Principles of Natural Philosophy*, tr. A. Motte 1729, revised F. Cajori, University of California Press 1962)

R. Norwood **10.1**, **10.2** (*The Seaman's Practice*)

Proclus **5.4***l* (*A Commentary on the First Book of Euclid's Elements*, tr. G.R. Morrow, Princeton University Press 1970)

R. Recorde 54*rt*, **9.1**, **9.2**, **9.3**, **9.5***lt*, **9.5***r* (*The Ground of Arts*); **9.4**, **F4***t*, **F4***lc* (*The Whetstone of Witte*)

G. Robins and C. Shute **2.1***lb* (*The Rhind Mathematical Papyrus*, British Museum Publications 1987)

A.J. Sjoberg **1.2***t* (*Journal of Cuneiform Studies*, 24 (1971/2), 127)

D.E. Smith **13.1**, **13.2** , **13.3**, **F5***lc*, **F5***lb* (adapted from *A Source Book in Mathematics*, McGraw-Hill 1929)

Martha Somerville 75–6, 76*lc* (*Personal Recollections of Mary Somerville (by her daughter)*, John Murray 1873)

F.J. Swetz and T.I. Kao **5.2**, **5.3** (adapted from *Was Pythagoras Chinese?*, Pennsylvania State University Press 1977)

E.G.R. Taylor (*The Mathematical Practitioners of Tudor and Stuart England*, Cambridge University Press 1954)

K. Vogel **7.1**, **7.2** (*Neun Bücher arithmetischer Technik*, Vieweg and Sohn, tr. F.R. Watson)

R.S. Westfall **14.1***t* (*Never at Rest: A Biography of Isaac Newton*, Cambridge University Press 1980)

Li Yan and Du Shiran 16*lb*, 17*lt*, 17*rb* (*Chinese Mathematics: A Concise History*, tr. J.N. Crossley and A.W.-C. Lun, Clarendon Press 1987)

The author and publisher would like to thank the following for permission to reproduce photographs and drawings.

Ashmolean Museum, Oxford 1

Robbie Bell cover (Queen Nefertari, National Museum, Cairo)

Marquis de Breteuil **15.1**

Bristol Museum and Art Gallery **9.2***t*, **9.2***ct*

British Library 45*l*, 45*r* (1487S1, Cardan, *De Subtilitate*); **12.3** (PP 2465, The *Ladies' Diary*)

© British Museum 5, **2.2***r*, **F1***tr*, **9.2***cb*, **9.2***b*, 78

British Museum Publications Ltd, © Gay Robins 10, **2.1** (Gay Robins and Charles Shute, *The Rhind Mathematical Papyrus*)

The Syndics of Cambridge University Library **F3**, 53*lc* (Recorde, *The Ground of Arts*); **8.2***t*, **8.3***t*, **8.4***c* (Babington, *A Short Treatise of Geometrie*); **9.1***tl*

The Syndicate of Cambridge University Press 16, **5.3***bl*, **7.1**, **7.2**, **8.4***b* (Needham, *Science and Civilisation in China*)

Rare Book and Manuscript Library, Columbia University **1.2a**

Mary Evans Picture Library **15.2**

Robert Harding Picture Library 24

The Mansell Collection 90

Metropolitan Museum of Art, The Carnarvon Collection, Gift of Edward S. Harkness, 1926 (26.7.1287) **F1***br*

National Maritime Museum London **10.1***c*

National Portrait Gallery, London 76

Oxford University Press **3.1** (Li Yan and Du Shiran, *Chinese Mathematics: A Concise History*)

The Pennsylvania State University Press **5.2**, **5.3***tr* (F. J. Swetz and T. I. Kao, *Was Pythagoras Chinese?*, University Park 1977), © 1977 The Pennsylvania State University, Reproduced by permission of the publisher.

Scottish Sunday Express, 20 June 1948, by courtesy of The Mitchell Library, Glasgow City Libraries **13.4***t*

Charles W. Turner Collection, Keele University cover, 61, 65, **11.1***t*, **11.1***c*, **11.2***c*, **11.2***b*, **11.3** (Leybourn, *Cursus Mathematicus*); 22 (Euclid, *Elements*); 43 (Mauro of Florence, *Spherae Mundi*); 45*ct* (Cardan, *Practica Arithmetica*); 45*cb* (Cardan, *De Artibus*); 47*t* (Moxon, *A tutor to Astronomie and Geographie*); **8.1***tl*, **8.1***tr*, **8.1***rct*, **8.1***rcb*, **8.1***lc*, **8.1***b* (Tartaglia, *Quesiti, et inventioni diverse ...*); **8.3***c*, **8.3***b*, **8.4***t* (S. Belli, *Libro del misurar con la vista ...*); 53; **9.1***cr*, **F4***t* (Recorde, *The Ground of Arts*); **9.3***t* (Menninger, *Number words and symbols*); **10.2** (Digges, *A Geometrical Practical Treatise named Pantometria*); **11.2***t* (Leybourn, *Arithmetick*); **11.5**, **11.7** (Mudge and Dalby, *An Account of the Operations Carried on for Accomplishing a Trigonometrical Survey of England and Wales*, Vol. 1, 1799); **14.1***t*, **14.1***c* (Newton, *Principia*); 94, **15.4***t* (Agnesi, *Institutioni Analitiche*); **F5** (Cardan, *Ars Magna*)

Introduction

A single volume about mathematics in history must necessarily leave out more than it includes. Foremost in choosing the content, I have looked for items of primary source material which are accessible to people of 10 years of age and upwards. The main point of such material is that it establishes direct contact with the past and is rich in all sorts of incidental information. It makes demands on the imagination, but trying to grasp and put oneself into a different style of thinking is all part of the fun! Do bear in mind that these are tiny extracts, sometimes drastically simplified and often in translation.

In the classroom sections suggest possible ways of working. The style is deliberately terse, so that you can consider the possibilities quickly. Most of the work relates to the main years of secondary schooling, that is to pupils in the 11–16 age range. Several pieces might be used with somewhat younger children, while some are definitely more suitable for students aged 16+. The curriculum index at the end of the book provides a guide to mathematical topics, and thus to the approximate level of each photocopiable sheet. No doubt you, the teacher, will dip in, pick out what seems useful, and pitch the work according to your classes.

The material is meant to promote active involvement, to allow pupils to work on, explore and develop some of the mathematics coming out of historical texts. Most likely this will be used in normal mathematics courses, but there is strong cross-curricular potential which history teachers and others may wish to exploit.

It seemed important to set the extracts in some sort of cultural context. Mathematics has not always been a compulsory subject of study for every child, nor of such recognized 'importance' in human affairs. Dipping into history naturally provides novelty, entertainment and interesting things to do. I hope it will also alert pupils to the different purposes for which mathematical kinds of knowledge have been used and to the different sorts of people who have written it down.

A Sumerian clay tablet from about 3000 BC. The scribe uses pictographic, pre-cuneiform symbols to record some details about food supplies.
(Ashmolean Museum, Oxford)

1

Background notes, given in each chapter, provide some good stories you can tell and, at the same time, I try to open up the context. This inevitably prompts more questions than I have space to tackle. Maybe, with the collaboration of other subject colleagues, you will be able to pursue some of these avenues.

To keep the task manageable, I decided to concentrate on two main historical threads, which are reflected in the general arrangement of the book.

Part 1 introduces some of our ancient civilizations, one in each of the first five chapters. Aspects of number, mensuration and geometry are developed. We can see the antiquity of much of the mathematics learned in school today. The need for it arose out of the greater complexity, especially in government and religion, of societies which were urbanized. Specialized training became necessary for those who would deal with food production and distribution, taxation, trade, inheritance, civic works and engineering.

Part 2 explores what may be loosely called the Renaissance to the Enlightenment in Europe. This period, of about 250 years, is particularly fertile in available material, suitable for school level and nicely exemplifying two important facets of mathematical endeavour. Scholars pushed back the frontiers of knowledge, and practitioners mastered basic mathematics and applied it to their occupations. Occupations illustrated here are gunnery, navigation and surveying.

The way of practitioners was not smooth. I include a folio sheet which indicates that traders in the Middle Ages were more likely to use finger numbers than to write numbers down. In chapter 9 we see that a book for adults needed to begin by explaining how to read and write numbers!

In the sixteenth century, mathematics was an all-male preserve, both for scholars and for artisans. By the eighteenth century, we can see the beginning of women's participation. This is considered in chapters 12 and 15.

Chapters 13 and 14 introduce probability theory and universal gravitation, two new ideas which symbolize a growing confidence in humankind's ability to explain and control the world.

For more mature pupils, some debate about the evolution of ideas may be appropriate. Today we take for granted a formalized, universal induction to knowledge and we aspire to the ideal of equal opportunities. Serious superstition is rare, we confidently predict, and we have faith in science. It was not always so, and the changes have their origins in history.

Folios, in both parts, are single, self-explanatory sheets. They can stand alone or they can fit into themes. Games of chance existed from antiquity, but it took the intellectual climate of the seventeenth century to prompt a mathematical treatment. Chinese magic squares serve to illustrate the wide and long-standing links between maths and magic. 'Twin lines' and 'Mental torture' demonstrate almost simultaneous developments, but at rather different levels, in the field of algebra.

The free-standing nature of the folios will, I hope, emphasize the dual nature of this book. It is possible to dip into any chapter for a quick resource, but there is also background and some recurring themes for those who want to follow them.

Answers to exercises are provided, along with notes, at the end of the book.

Part 1 Mathematics in antiquity

Some five or six millennia ago, a few of the simple farming communities in the world began to change. Agriculture became efficient enough to support an urban population and, in several places, writing was invented. Mechanisms of government were needed to maintain an ordered society and to direct the communal effort required to sustain it. Societies could also support a full-time priesthood with a range of functions. As prosperity grew, so did many other features of civilized life such as the skilled arts, trade, literature, scholarship and mathematics.

Written numbers were obviously important for recording, keeping account of events and of supplies and of taxes. Methods were devised for doing calculations. Astronomy, linked to the creation of a calendar, added impetus to the development of mathematics of both a numerical and a geometrical kind. Developing religious ritual could have a similar effect. Both shared an interest in predicting and possibly controlling events: the time for sowing, the coming of rains, the fate of cities and so on. Geometry and mensuration also have practical roots in surveying and building.

People who could write and who practised the art are generally known as scribes. It took time and effort to learn the scribal art, and hence the invention of schools. Once founded, schools provided the spur for further organization and for the development of knowledge which went beyond the merely utilitarian. This is clear from some of the esoteric problems in texts which survive. Dipping into ancient mathematics reveals that many of the mathematical ideas taught in school today were already well developed in those early times.

It is worth remembering that all this took place before the advent of paper. These are some of the writing materials used:

Mesopotamia: clay tablets, wedge-shaped marks made by pressing a stylus into the damp clay.

Egypt: rock inscriptions in hieroglyphics; on papyrus and leather, writing with pen and ink.

China: early writing cut into bones, shells and pottery, then ink on bamboo strips; main early mathematical work known through later copies on paper; silk also used as writing material.

India: pictographic symbols on stone seals, later writing on bark or palm leaves according to region; early mathematics communicated orally.

Greece: writing on waxed boards, reused for short or temporary material; papyrus rolls for 'permanence'; only late copies and translations survive.

Writing in the sand was common in many places.

Some early civilizations

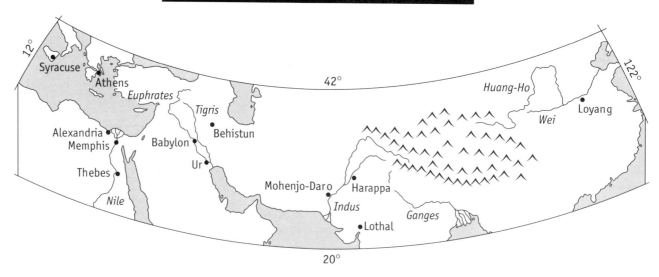

BC	Mesopotamia	Egypt and Mediterranean		India	China
3000	*Sumerian cities* Sexagesimal numbers and cuneiform	*Pharaohs rule united Egypt* Hieroglyphics Pyramids	Megalithic temples on Malta	*Harappan cities*	
2500	*Semitic influx* and Akkadian language				*Xia Dynasty* and Legendary Yu
		The Old Kingdom			
2000	*Babylonian rule* Maths excellence	Moscow papyrus Leather roll Rhind papyrus	*Minoan civilization on Crete*	*Aryan influx* Hinduism *Vedic period*	*Shang Dynasty* Oracle bone numerals
1500	*Various rulers from Hittite ...*	*The New Kingdom*			
				Sulbasutras	*Zhou Dynasty*
1000		Greek city states developing			
	... to Assyrian Science thriving			Jainism	'Modern' numerals
500	*Persian Empire and Darius*	Thales and Pythagoras *Rising Roman power* Athenian schools		Sanskrit grammar ·Buddhism	Confucius Mencius
		← *Alexandrian Empire* →			*Qin* and book burning
0 AD		Euclid and Archimedes *Roman Empire* Ptolemy		*Maurya Empire and* Brahmi numerals	*Han Dynasty* and Mathematical classics
250	Astronomy thriving			Bakhshali manuscript	*Jin Dynasty* and Liu Hui

Multiplying in Babylon

Briefing

Cuneiform numerals are introduced by decoding clay tablet multiplication tables, suitable for all ages. Features of base sixty are explored, including simple division with units of time and money. This may be taken at a more advanced level to include reciprocals and 'sexagesimal fractions'.

Background

A broad plain lies between two great rivers which rise in the mountains of Armenia and flow their separate ways to the Persian Gulf. Known in the past as Mesopotamia, this is the region of modern-day Iraq. By 3000 BC, the endemic floods and droughts were being mastered by irrigation, bronze ploughs were in use, and cities of unprecedented size were flourishing in the southern area. The Sumerian people, who had started to write in a pictographic script, began to develop a more versatile system and came to use the wedge-shaped characters known as cuneiform.

The cities tended to battle between themselves and suffered various incursions from surrounding peoples, but despite the spates of battling and destruction, knowledge was passed on and libraries grew. We read in the book of Genesis how Abraham set out from the city of Ur to found the Jewish nation. Excavations at Ur have revealed a city of splendid temples and rich tombs. Delicate ornaments of precious stones and a wonderfully decorated gold helmet are amongst its treasures.

By 1800 BC, it was the Amorite city of Babylon which gained ascendancy over the whole region under its king, Hammurabi. Hammurabi is perhaps most famous for his code of laws, though his was certainly not the first code. Hammurabi's code is carved on a two-metre-high pillar of black rock, now housed in the Louvre with a copy in the British Museum. His laws prescribe severe punishments for crime on the basis of 'an eye for an eye'. They also promote fair dealing by governing wages and commerce and carefully protect the rights of all, including women, children and slaves. There was obviously much well-rewarded work in civic and commercial fields for the trained scribe, some recompense perhaps for a tough school life where beatings seem to have been common.[1]

The Babylonians also used the cuneiform script and wrote in the Sumerian style with a shaped reed pressed into soft clay. This could later be baked in the sun or in a kiln. Huge quantities of clay tablets have been unearthed. The mathematical ones from the Old Babylonian era are particularly plentiful and interesting. The numbers are relatively easy to read, operating on a place value principle in the base of sixty. Thus 1,7 means sixty and seven; but

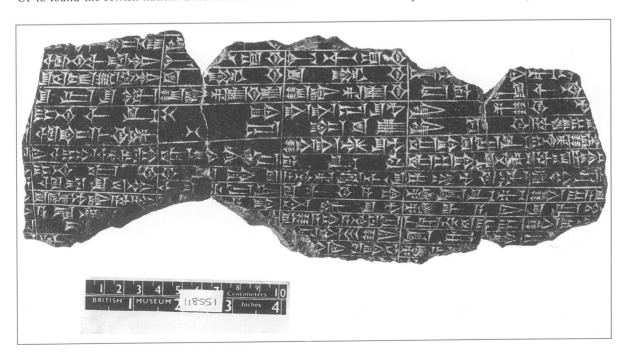

Detail of a cuneiform inscription from Hammurabi's time.

you may also come across 21, 49 meaning 21 sixties and 49 units which we can transcribe into decimal as 1260 + 49 or 1309. Units of measurement were also sexagesimal, although sometimes they had an intermediate ten or six grouping: for instance the 360 degrees in a circle is six sixties.

Deciphering the written word, when the spoken languages were lost, proved a more intricate problem. Success was eventually achieved after a British diplomat, on rock-climbing weekends in southern Iran, copied out ancient inscriptions from a sheer cliff face. The monument on which he worked is at Behistun.[2] It celebrates the exploits of Darius the Great in three different languages. By careful comparison between them, the wedge-shaped script of ancient Babylon was eventually decoded.

In the classroom

Decode the tables tablets

The number system is not difficult to decipher from scratch, so why not begin with some detective work? Copies of **sheet 1.1** should be cut up to represent a collection of clay tablets found in the desert. Better still of course, if you know a cooperative potter, make some real tablets. Later on, pupils can experiment with writing in clay themselves. A spatula or shaped dowel makes authentic wedge marks when pressed in at the correct angles. It is important to press, rather than to scratch the surface; the action is different from using a pen.

Whether you have tablets then, or have reproduced the drawings, distribute them and allow time for pupils to try to make sense of what is written. Discoveries are gradually made and word soon gets around that these are times tables.

Detectives reporting. On the 2×, 3× and 5× tables tablets, you appear to have a base ten system, with repetition of ▮ for units, and of ◀ for tens. On the 6×, 8× and 9× tablets, something strange happens at sixty and above. Pupils can try to resolve it, and then go on to write some numbers of their own 'in Babylonian style'. Someone's height, say 134 centimetres, consists of two sixties and fourteen and so would be written ▮▮◀▮▮▮.

Write more tables. As a collaborative project, the class could construct a set of tables for 4× (no problem), 7×, 10×, 12×, 15×, 16×, 18× or 20×. All of these, and more, have actually been found on surviving tablets. If pupils ask about a sign for zero, you can tell them that it was not introduced for more than a thousand years; in 1800 BC scribes simply left a gap. Still remaining authentically Babylonian, they might try making tables of squares, cubes, or compound interest at different rates!

Practise transcribing. The tablet reproduced at the top of **sheet 1.2** is famous for its contents, which we shall explore in chapter 5, 'Background'. At this stage it is useful simply to show the genuine appearance of wedge marks and to introduce some large numbers. In the left-hand column there are some apparently huge numbers; in the right-hand column the numbers from 1 to 4 and from 7 to 13 can be distinguished. It is best to start with the middle two columns. In the first row of these we read 1,59 and 2,49. Translated into our decimal notation they mean 119 and 169. On the next line we find 56,7 and then 3,12,1 which is presumably a three-place sexagesimal number. If so, its value is 3×60^2 plus 12×60 plus 1. The middle columns on the third line translate to 4601 and 6649.

Delights of dividing in base sixty

As pupils have become acquainted with the number system, it seems a pity to leave without attempting to appreciate the virtues of base sixty for calculations. A simple start can be made with sharing out. Pieces of silver generally served for money and were measured by weight, 60 shekels being worth 1 mana, and 60 mana 1 talent. If 7 talents is divided equally between different groups of people, we get the following results – the division becoming harder with 8 or 9 people:

Number of people	Amount	
2	3 talents,	30 mana
3	2 talents,	20 mana
4	1 talent,	45 mana
5	1 talent,	24 mana
6	1 talent,	10 mana
7	1 talent	
8	52 mana,	30 shekels
9	46 mana,	40 shekels
10	42 mana	

At 11 'it won't divide' as some of the scribes have written, but observe that with pounds or dollars we should run into that problem much earlier. £7 cannot be divided exactly by 3, 6, 8 or 9. The number 60 is blessed with many more factors than the number 100.

Try some similar problems dividing a number of hours into minutes and seconds, a division of time in which the whole world has been influenced by Mesopotamian civilization.

If you work out divisions of 1 hour systematically, dividing in turn by 2, by 3, by 4, etc., you will produce results which begin to look like the tablet transcribed on **sheet 1.2b**:

1 hour divided by 2 would be 30 minutes

1 hour divided by 3 would be 20 minutes and so on.

In the second column:

1 hour divided by 16 would be 3 minutes, 45 seconds.

Several tablets with these same results have been unearthed,[3] suggesting that they played an important part in Babylonian arithmetic. We can see, for instance, how this tablet might have served as a ready reckoner for sharing 7 talents equally between 16 people. From the table:

1 talent divided by 16 gives 3 mana, 45 shekels

so

7 talents divided by 16 gives 3,45 times 7

and this product could be looked up in a multiplication table!

What if you need to divide by 11 or by one of the other numbers which 'won't divide' exactly? The Babylonians were prepared to give an answer to the nearest approximation.

A more demanding extension

Follow up with the use of this table (**sheet 1.2b**) for pure sexagesimal numbers.[4] It provides a basis for any type of fractional calculation, not just in money and time.

We have already seen that working out $\frac{7}{16}$ is done as $7 \times (\frac{1}{16})$. The table tells us that $\frac{1}{16}$ of an hour is 3 minutes 45 seconds, or that $\frac{1}{16}$ of a talent is 3 mana, 45 shekels. In more abstract terms, $\frac{1}{16}$ of 1 (unit) is no units, 3 of the next smaller unit and 45 of the next smaller unit. This we could write as 0;3,45, though in Old Babylonian times the zero would be 'understood' rather than written. Thought of as pure number, this is a 'sexagesimal' fraction comparable to our 'decimals'.

In this sense the tablet is simply a reciprocal table. To divide by a number, you multiply by its reciprocal.

The supposition that Babylonians coped with fractions in this efficient way is supported by the existence of multiplication tablets for every one of the numbers occurring in the reciprocal table.[5]

Thus to work out $\frac{10}{81}$ as sexagesimal, you only have to look up two tables. First of all, look for 1,21 (the Babylonian for eighty-one) in the reciprocal table. You get in effect 0;0,44,26,40. Then turn to the multiplication table for 44,26,40 where you read off the tenth multiple, 7,24,26,4. This is your answer, consisting of four sexagesimal places! It means, in our notation,

$$\frac{7}{60} + \frac{24}{(60)^2} + \frac{26}{(60)^3} + \frac{4}{(60)^4}$$

whereas we would write 0.1234 ... meaning

$$\frac{1}{10} + \frac{2}{(10)^2} + \frac{3}{(10)^3} + \frac{4}{(10)^4} \quad ....$$

Daunting to the beginner, it nevertheless repays further study. Certainly the astronomers of the West found it so; Copernicus was using sexagesimal parts in the sixteenth century AD.

Babylonian clay tablets

1.2a

Babylon around 1600 BC

'Work hard at the scribal art and it will bring you riches.'

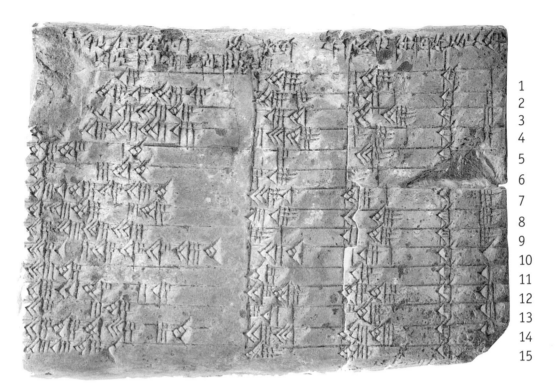

1
2
3
4
5
6
7
8
9
10
11
12
13
14
15

Babylonian tablet number 322 from the Plimpton collection, Columbia University

1.2b

A commonly used table in Old Babylonia

Numbers are in base sixty.

2	30	16	3,45	45	1,20
3	20	18	3,30	48	1,15
4	15	20	3	50	1,12
5	12	24	2,30	54	1, 6,40
6	10	25	2,24	1	1
8	7,30	27	2,13,20	1,4	56,15
9	6,40	30	2	1,12	50
10	6	32	1,52,30	1,15	48
12	5	36	1,40	1,20	45
15	4	40	1,30	1,21	44,26,40

Doubling in Egypt

Briefing

The Egyptian system of long multiplication, based on doubling, has appeal for anyone who finds difficulty in remembering their tables. Practice in using it in the context of typical scribal tasks is given.

Tabulated unit fractions occur in several surviving sources. One of these, in hieratic script, is offered for decoding and leads to some open questions about fraction combinations.

Background

Civilized life under the Pharaohs in Egypt lasted for two thousand years, very little disturbed by warfare. There was a brief period when the Hyksos, a better-armed people from the east, swept in to dominate the Delta region. This followed a period of weakened administration known as the Middle Kingdom, which in its turn had followed the demise of the Old Kingdom in uncharacteristic civil strife. The Hyksos were soon challenged by people of Thebes in Upper Egypt, that long valley stretching south to the first cataract of the Nile. The success of the Theban campaign, in about 1600 BC, enabled a new succession of Pharaohs to unite the country and establish a regime of more imperialist character, which flourished for another 500 years. This New Kingdom was the time of Tutankhamun and the royal tombs in the remote 'Valley of the Kings'.

The Old Kingdom, from roughly 3000 to 2200 BC, was that amazing era when the pyramids were built, not only to serve as royal tombs but as monuments to the highly ordered state which could create them. The Nile, on which all depended, set a rhythm to the year. From July to September was the Inundation, when the water rose to flood and refresh all the low-lying areas. This became a time when the peasantry were conscripted to labour on great building works. Then came the Emergence, when they returned to plough the land, sow crops and attend to irrigation. By February the harvest was ready and government officials set out across the land to collect Pharaoh's designated share, or rather to collect what was regarded as Pharaoh's, leaving behind a share for those who had produced it! When all was complete, building and other public works could begin again.

Tax dues were all carefully worked out after measuring the height of the year's flood on a rock stairway constructed at the head of the valley. Clearly there was much work for scribes to do in assessing estates for productivity, apportioning supplies to officials and foremen and in all the meticulous record-keeping which characterized Egyptian life. It was an arduous training, probably twelve years from dawn to dusk in the temple school, but in a stratified society it offered the hope of advancement.

The well-known hieroglyphic script was normally used on monuments, but a more cursive script known as 'hieratic' was soon developed for everyday writing. The papyrus reeds which served for raft and boat building also yielded flat strips of pith. These were placed in two layers at right angles, moistened, pounded and dried, to produce an excellent writing surface. The scribe's equipment included reed pens with black and red inks.

The major sources for our knowledge of Egyptian mathematics are two surviving papyrus rolls which were actually written during the Middle Kingdom and Hyksos periods. It seems most likely that the methods contained were known in earlier times. The first is now in Moscow and the second, known as the Rhind Mathematical Papyrus (RMP), is in the British Museum with some fragments of it in the Brooklyn Museum, New York. The RMP is a 5-metre roll, 32 cm in height, consisting of sheets of papyrus gummed together and written on both sides. It came to light in the 1850s when a young lawyer, Henry Rhind, purchased it from a trader in Luxor.

The writer of RMP gives his name as Ahmose and says that he is copying an earlier work. For $1\frac{1}{2}$ metres on the front of the roll, he sets out a table of fractions. Then, often using these, he solves 87 problems of different types.[1] The opening words of each problem are in red ink and the main part of the method in black. Rhind also acquired a much smaller roll of leather which was so fragile that it

Scribe at work.

could not be unrolled until 1927 when techniques had developed sufficiently. That too lists some relations between fractions.

The need for these fraction tables is connected with the Egyptian methods for multiplication and division, which were based on doubling and halving. To multiply a number by 5, you doubled, doubled again and added the original number. Alternatively, since the numerals were in base ten, it was easy to multiply by 10, so you could multiply the number by 10 and then halve it. Thus for 320×5 you could set it out in either of the following ways. The pieces which are added to make the total are shown in **bold** type.

1	**320**		1	320
2	640		10	3200
4	**1280**		**5**	**1600**
Total	1600		Total	1600

The answer incidentally tells you that there would be 1600 ro in 5 hekats! One ro was the smallest unit for measuring grain, about a heaped dessertspoonful, and a hekat was the large dry measure for grain, roughly 5 litres. There were 320 ro to a hekat.

Fractions tended to occur in the numerous sharing by proportion problems and were always expressed as unit fractions (except for $\frac{2}{3}$). Thus to share out 4 loaves equally between 9 people, the answer was not $\frac{4}{9}$ of a loaf as we should say, but a third of a loaf for each person (using up 3 loaves) and then one-ninth of the loaf that was left. So according to Egyptian thinking, 4 divided by 9 is $\frac{1}{3} + \frac{1}{9}$. Now to double this quantity (say for a double ration), double $\frac{1}{3}$ to get $\frac{2}{3}$ and double $\frac{1}{9}$. But here is the tricky part: you have to think in terms of unit fractions, i.e. single portions of a particular size, and not in terms of $\frac{2}{9}$. Here the scribe could look up in his table (or remember) that $\frac{1}{9}$ is equal to $\frac{1}{12} + \frac{1}{36}$ and so doubling a $\frac{1}{9}$ portion gives $\frac{1}{6} + \frac{1}{18}$. Doubling that quantity could be done again very easily because both the denominators are even. The table in the Rhind papyrus gives the double of all the odd fractions up to $\frac{1}{101}$.

In transcribing, it is normal to write Egyptian fractions with a bar; thus $\overline{101}$ for $\frac{1}{101}$ and $\overline{\overline{3}}$ for $\frac{2}{3}$.

In the classroom

Long multiplication Egyptian style

You might like to demonstrate with the example given above, or with the following computation which works out quantities required to supply a class of 33 pupils with a can of coke each day for a month of 31 days!

Two possible layouts for calculating 33×31 are:

1	31		1	33
2	62		**10**	**330**
4	124		**20**	**660**
8	248			
16	496		Total	1023
32	**992**			
Total	1023			

The general principle is to double or to multiply by ten. Encourage the pupils to choose intelligently.

Pupils can attempt questions 1–6 on **sheet 2.1.** (The answers are given in 'Notes on sheets', at the end of the book.) They may be interested in some background about ancient Egypt. For fun, some of the text is given in hieroglyphs. The basic symbols for units, tens, hundreds, etc. are repeated the requisite number of times. Thus ∩∩'''' means 27 and 999|| means 302. Strictly these should be written in the reverse order, reading from right to left. Although easy to interpret, they are tedious to write. If pupils try, they will soon realize why the hieratic symbols were developed for everyday writing.

Units for grain measure were given earlier. For length, the units were commonly 4 fingerbreadths to a palm, 7 palms to a cubit and 100 cubits to a khet. Bread and beer were indeed the staple commodities and, in the absence of coinage, were normally used for payments. A hand-fed goose, roasted on a spit, seems to have been a popular dish at feasts held in the homes of the wealthy.

The multiplication method was adapted for division. Suppose you ask the question, 'How long would 605 cans last 33 of us?' You can find the answer by building up from 33 until you can put together pieces totalling 605. In this case it becomes necessary to take a fraction, $\frac{1}{3}$ of 33, which we write in imitation of the hieroglyph as $\overline{3}$.

Start like this:

1	33
2	66
4	132
8	264
16	528

Clearly to double again would take us too far, so let us see what we can do with what we have:

1	33
2	**66**
4	132
8	264
16	**528**

Trying out totals gives:

18	594

This means that we need 11, which added to 594 makes 605. This can be done by taking one third of the first line:

3̄	**11**

Adding the three parts gives:

18 3̄	605

605 cans would give 33 pupils a can a day for $18\frac{1}{3}$ days.

Questions 7–11 on **sheet 2.1** offer some practice.

Sheet 2.2 Working with fractions

A section of Rhind's leather roll is reproduced on this sheet. It contains nine lines of hieratic script, each one stating a sum of unit fractions. Egyptologists were rather disappointed when the roll was eventually opened to find just four columns of these fractions. It remains a puzzle why the scribe wrote on such a valuable material.

Pupils should try to read and check each line of this costly document. Remind them to pay special attention to the dots: ıııı means 4 but ıııı means $\frac{1}{4}$. Even worse ∴ means 40 but ∴ means $\frac{1}{40}$. Then for $\frac{1}{44}$ you put the dot over the forty only, giving ıııı∴ because you must read from right to left. The first line of the text contains the sum of three fractions, as shown in the diagram at the bottom of the page.

There is no + sign and no = sign, but as the three fractions on the right do add up to $\frac{1}{15}$ it is clear what was meant. In each of the following lines there are just two fractions added.

Follow-on possibilities

1 The combinations are not listed in a systematic order on the roll, but if pupils pick out $\frac{1}{64}$, $\frac{1}{32}$, $\frac{1}{16}$, perhaps they can then suggest pairs which add to $\frac{1}{8}$, $\frac{1}{4}$, $\frac{1}{2}$ and check them by normal fraction addition.

2 Can pupils work out combinations for $\frac{1}{6}$ and $\frac{1}{18}$, which are also missing from this column?

3 In the totals column, the only odd denominator given is 15, but in Egyptian arithmetic it was particularly useful to be able to express 'odd' fractions in terms of 'even' ones. Elsewhere $\frac{1}{15}$ is considered as $\frac{1}{20} + \frac{1}{60}$. This has the advantage that you can easily double $\frac{1}{15}$ whilst keeping the answer in terms of unit fractions. You get $\frac{1}{10} + \frac{1}{30}$ rather than our form $\frac{2}{15}$. In fact this combination is so good that you can double again to get $\frac{1}{5} + \frac{1}{15}$ in place of $\frac{4}{15}$. This ability to double was crucial in Egyptian multiplication and division. Pupils could try to find similar 'even' pairs for $\frac{1}{5}$, $\frac{1}{7}$, $\frac{1}{9}$, ... and work out the double (and quadruple?) of each. It may be helpful to remember that $\frac{1}{3} = \frac{1}{4} + \frac{1}{12}$.

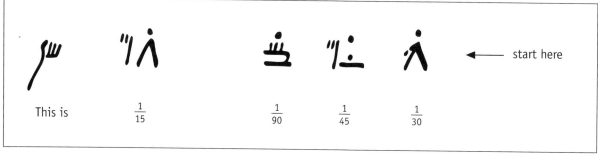

This is $\frac{1}{15}$ $\frac{1}{90}$ $\frac{1}{45}$ $\frac{1}{30}$ ← start here

How to read the leather roll.

Some tasks for an Egyptian scribe

Hieroglyphics		
Find	𓅯	
1	∣	
10	∩	
100	𓏲	a coil of rope
1000	𓆼	a lotus flower
10 000		
100 000		
1 000 000		The god of air and space (little used)
a half		
a quarter		

I   A hekat of barley makes ∣∣∣ jugs of beer. 𓅯 jugs from ∩∩∣∣∣∣ hekats.

II   A hekat of flour makes ∣∣∣∣∣ loaves of bread. 𓅯 loaves from ∩∣∣ hekats.

III   𓆼𓆼𓆼𓏲𓏲𓏲∩∩∩ ∩∩ bricks to make a ramp. 𓅯 bricks for ∣∣∣∣∣∣ ramps.

IIII   A field of breadth ∩∩∩∩∩ cubits, length 𓏲∩∩ cubits, 𓅯 area.

IIIII   Fattening ∣∣∣∣∣∣∣∣ geese, each gets ∣∣∣∣∣∣∣∣∣∣ ro grain a day, 𓅯 grain for ∩ days.

IIIIII   An army unit needs ∩∩∣∣∣∣∣ loaves and ∩∩∩∣∣∣∣∣ jugs of beer a day. 𓅯 supplies for an ∩∣∣∣∣∣ day mission.

IIIIIII   A herdsman has ∩∩∩∣∣∣∩∩∣∣∣ cattle. He must pay a quarter in tax. How many cows should the tax collector take?

IIIIIIII   Share a 𓏲∩∩∩∣∣∣∣∩∩∩ palm length of cloth equally between ∩∣∣ servants.

IIIIIIIII   𓏲∩∩∩∣∣∣ jugs of beer for ∩∩∩∣∣∣ men, but the boatman gets a double share. How many jugs each?

∩   The temple director gets ∩ portions, ∣∣∣ priests get ∣∣∣∣∣ each, two guards and the scribe get ∣ each, and ∣∣∣∣ workers get ◡ each. 𓅯 their shares from 𓏲𓏲∩∩∣∣∣∩∩∣∣∣ ro of fat.

∩∣   A hekat of flour makes ∩∣∣∣∣ loaves, how much flour for a loaf every day for a year?

'See, I am instructing you ...
so that you may become one who
is trusted by the king, so that
you may take delivery from the
corn-bearing ships at the
entrance to the granary, so
that on feast days you may
measure out the god's offerings.'

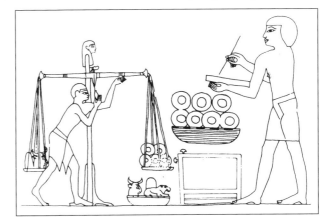

A scribe records the weight of gold; from a tomb at Thebes

Know your hieratic

Hieratic numerals

1	$\mid$	10	
2	$\mid\mid$	20	
3	$\mid\mid\mid$	30	
4	$\mid\mid\mid\mid$	40	
5		50	
6		60	
7		70	
8		80	
9		90	
		100	

means 'This is'

Part of the Egyptian leather roll

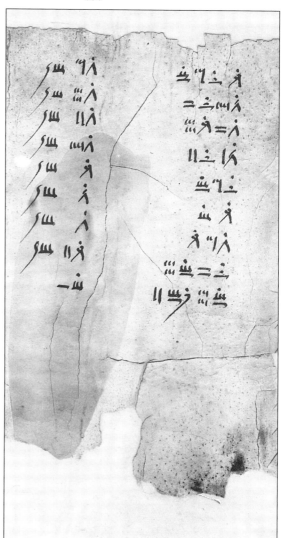

Reading fractions

A dot over 7, makes it $^1/_7$.

A dot over 60, makes it $^1/_{60}$, and so on.

Numbers are written from right to left, and with just one dot for each fraction,

so means $^1/_{67}$

and means $^1/_{192}$.

Games of chance

People enjoyed games of chance, and soothsayers cast lots, from very early times. Not until the seventeenth century was a theory of chance properly developed. Even today, players hold on to superstitions and ideas of luck which may be contrary to mathematical advice!

We are used to unbiased dice, but people often played with more irregular objects such as a bone from the heel of a sheep (an *astragalus*). In the Roman Empire, gambling took such a hold that it was officially banned except at the feast of Saturn each December. Several emperors seem to have ignored the ban! In one popular game, you had to roll four *astragali* together. Each *astragalus* could fall on four distinct faces. The most valuable throw, called a Venus throw, happened when a different face showed up on each of the four *astragali* (illustrated below).

Part of a Sumerian board game made of lapis lazuli, shell and red limestone set in bitumen, *c*. 2500 BC

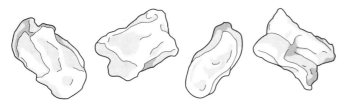

Animal bones, called *astragali*, used as dice

- You could plan a game with either regular or irregular objects. Then try to work out the probabilities of some different combinations.

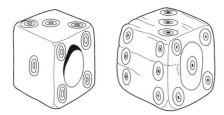

Roman dice

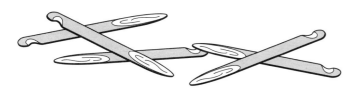

Throwing sticks, sometimes used like dice to decide moves in a game

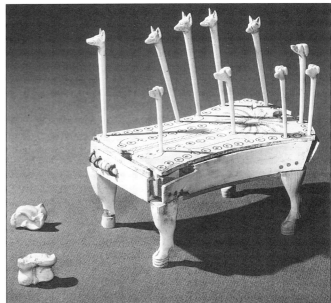

An ivory game from an Egyptian tomb *c*. 1800 BC. Teams of hounds and jackals race around a palm tree. All rights reserved, The Metropolitan Museum of Art.

Bamboo in China

Briefing

Chinese number symbols have hardly changed in two thousand years. Decipher multiplication tables from ancient bamboo strips and see how the counting board was used. Positive and negative numbers were represented by different types of rod; add and subtract them in Chinese style.

Background

Some core part of the region known as China today has, until this century, generally been ruled by a royal house or dynasty. Dynasties have been overthrown by invasion or by internal conflict, and boundaries and capitals have changed. There has sometimes been a period of disunity, such as the 'Warring States Period', before another dynasty has established itself, but the thread of civilization has been continuous from its beginning. Because of this living tradition, legends are known which tell of the distant past. They can sometimes, but not always, be authenticated by archaeological evidence.

During the third millenium BC village communities began to thrive on the strange loess terraces above the Yellow River. This loess is a fertile yellow dust, blown from the Gobi Desert. It is told that about 2200 BC Yu the Great, founding emperor of the Xia Dynasty, succeeded in harnessing the fickle Yellow River by means of great ditches, dykes and reservoirs. By these means, the huge flood plain of the river became available for expanding settlements.

The Xia Dynasty was succeeded by the Shang, which lasted from about the 16th to the 11th century BC. From this period, physical remains of writing have been found. Brief records were incised into bones and the under-shells of tortoises. For example, 'The eighth day, 2656 men were killed while crossing spears', or after a hunting exploit, '56 deer'.[1]

The Zhou Dynasty came next. During this time Confucius and Mencius lived and the classical books were written. Duties and ranks of government officials were highly designated. The following instructions are recorded for education:

> Teach the six-year-olds numbers and directions ... the nine-year-olds how to work out days and dates. The ten-year-olds study with a teacher and live away from home learning history, writing, and mathematics.[2]

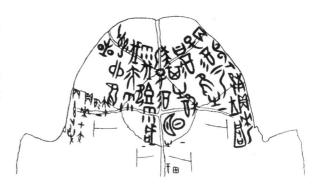

An inscription on the under-shell of a turtle from *c*. 1300 BC. It mentions the bright red star in our constellation of Hydra, called in Chinese the Bird Star.

Next the vigorous Qin emperor unified China, completed the first building of the Great Wall and standardized weights, measures and the writing of Chinese characters. Alas, in 213 BC he ordered 'the burning of the books'. Knowledge, and probably a few of the books, did, however, survive his short dynasty (221 BC to 206 BC).

During the following Han Dynasty (206 BC to AD 220), agriculture, trade, bureaucracy, technology and culture all flourished. Strips of bamboo, silk and wood were all being used as writing materials, and paper was invented.

Clearly it is difficult to date the origin of mathematical ideas, but by the Han Dynasty geometrical knowledge and a high level of computational skill were well established, probably having emerged much earlier. Calculations were normally done with the aid of short sticks of bamboo, bone or other material laid out on a counting board. The board was divided into columns for units, tens, hundreds and so on. The counting rods were set out in the columns in particular patterns to represent the digits, so that the layout of the board represented a place-value system of numeration.

Those doing the calculations would write down only the answer: their working was done by moving the rods! Techniques were available for extracting roots to any desired accuracy and for solving simultaneous equations in three or four unknowns. Whilst multiplication could obviously be done with the rods, it seems that the learning of multiplication tables was encouraged. Many bamboo and wood strips engraved with traces of the tables have been excavated in North West China and are commonly known as Han strips.

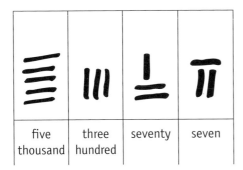

five thousand	three hundred	seventy	seven

Units are vertical, tens are horizontal,
hundreds stand, thousands lie down;
Thousands and tens look the same,
ten thousands and hundreds look alike;
When you reach six,
Five is on top.

Counting board and rhyme.

The most influential mathematics text from ancient China is the *Jiuzhang suanshu*. We shall also dip into the *Zhoubi suanjing*. This has been colourfully translated as *The Arithmetical Classic of the Gnomon and the Circular Paths of Heaven*.

Pinyin is the standard method for transcribing Chinese characters today. Less recent books often use the Wade–Giles system, so that you may find 九章算術 transcribed as Jiŭzhāng suànshù (Pinyin) or as Chiu Chang Suan Shu (Wade–Giles). A rough guide to pronunciation is included on sheet 3.1. To pronounce vowels more accurately you need to take account of the marks which indicate the tone of voice: ¯ flat, ´ rising, ˇ dipping, ` dropping.[3] At least in the case of the *Jiuzhang suanshu* there is consensus about the translation; it is known as the *Nine Chapters on the Mathematical Art*.

These nine chapters contain a total of 246 problems with their solutions given as exemplars. They were probably compiled, by an unknown author, during the Han Dynasty. The work represents the culmination and systematization of the mathematics which had been developed up to that time. Thereafter it was copied many times and commentators elaborated it in their own ways. Perhaps the most influential commentator was Liu Hui,[4] who lived about AD 250. He wrote explanations and proofs to go with some of the standard methods. Works of Liu Hui and the *Nine Chapters* were included in prescribed texts for more than a thousand years. The earliest edition of the *Jiuzhang* to physically survive comes from the thirteenth century AD. By this time books were being printed in China.

In the classroom

Chinese times tables, or the nine-nines rhyme

Sheet 3.1 portrays the legible part of a Han bamboo strip. Pupils may be able to make guesses about the meaning of some of the symbols, or you can give them the guide on the other part of the sheet. Even then the meaning of the strip may not be clear if pupils are reading across from left to right. Look, however, at the first block of numbers and read down in columns, starting from the top right corner:

7	8	9
9	9	9
6	7	8
10	10	10
3	2	1

This should surely be interpreted, 'Nine nines are eight tens and one, eight nines are seven tens and two' etc.

If pupils need some tables practice, you may want them to fill in the parts which have been obliterated over the 2000 years the strip was buried. Children in China today still learn this by heart as the nines-nines rhyme. There are also several interesting features to notice: a place value system in base ten is used consistently, but with the place values, i.e. the ten, hundred, etc., written in (except that there are abbreviations for twenty, thirty and forty). The tables obviously start at 9×9 and work down, but the eight-times table starts at 8×8, and so on. It is intriguing that having done 8×9 in the nine-times table, no need was felt for 9×8. Neither are any ten-times or one-times included at this early date.

When we say 3×2 and 2×3, we are doing basically the same thing. How many of these repeats do we learn? How do pupils think the Chinese managed without the $10 \times$ table?

There is a story[5] from the so-called Spring and Autumn Period (770–476 BC) which suggests that the tables were well known in China by that time. Duke Huan wanted to establish a distinguished academy, but after a year no one had applied for a job. Then a man brought along the 'nine-nines rhyme' as a gift for the Duke and to show off his knowledge! Duke Huan thought it was quite a joke, but the man said, 'As a matter of fact, knowing the nine-nines rhyme is nothing special, but if you appoint me there is no doubt that more outstanding people will queue up for employment.' And so it proved to be.

The column of symbols at the bottom of the strip means, 'The total is 1110.' There is worthwhile mathematics in trying to find short cuts to check this. In other words, look for easy methods to add up all of these products:

$$(9 \times 9) + (8 \times 9) + (7 \times 9) + \dots\dots\dots\dots\dots + (2 \times 9)$$
$$+ (8 \times 8) + (7 \times 8) + \dots\dots\dots\dots\dots + (2 \times 8)$$
$$+ (7 \times 7) + \dots\dots\dots\dots\dots + (2 \times 7)$$
$$\dots\dots$$
$$+ (3 \times 3) + (2 \times 3)$$
$$+ (2 \times 2)$$

Gaining and spending with counters

In Far Eastern markets today you can often see an abacus used for calculation. The abacus is the successor to the ancient Chinese counting board. Rather than trying to learn specific details or techniques, focus on one remarkable feature: the use of different kinds of rod for positive and negative numbers.

People used square section or black rods for what was paid out or a deficit, triangular section or red rods for receipts or a positive balance. The concept of positive and negative numbers with rules for adding and subtracting them was clearly formulated in China at least 1500 years before it was done in Europe.[6] Rules for multiplication and division came very much later (appearing in a book, Suanxue Qimeng, about AD 1300).

For pupils, experience with any two distinct types of counter can provide a useful conceptual foundation.

Suppose we take, for example, red Lego blocks for gains (+) and similar black blocks for losses (−):

Gained 7, spent 5	2 better off
Gained 2, spent 8	6 worse off
Spent 9, spent 5	14 worse off

and so on.

This adding of positive and negative is straightforward, but helps to establish that *any red-and-black pair is worth zero* and thus paves the way for subtracting:

$^-6$, take away $^-1$

$^-5$ is left.

But if you have $^+6$ (6 reds), you cannot physically take away $^-1$ (one black). The way to achieve this is to add zero, in the form of a red-and-black pair. Six reds then becomes 7 reds and a black. Then you can take the 1 black away, leaving 7 reds (that is, $^+7$).

'$^+6$, take away $^-3$' requires putting an extra 3 of the red-and-black pairs (still equivalent to zero) onto the table.

$^+6$, take away $^-3$

$^+6$, add zero, take away $^-3$

$^+6$, add ($^+3$ and $^-3$), take away $^-3$

$^+6$, add $^+3$ and ($^-3$ take away $^-3$)

$^+9$

Plenty of experience with counters will help to make sense of the rules for adding and subtracting with positive and negative quantities. It certainly did so very early in the development of Chinese arithmetic.

Writing on bamboo

2000-year-old bamboo strip (an enlarged drawing)

one	一	yi
two	二	er
three	三	san
four	四	si
five	五	wu
six	六	liu
seven	七	qi
eight	八	ba
nine	九	jiu
ten	十	shi
hundred	百	bai
thousand	千	qian

The writer of the bamboo strip used special symbols for

twenty

thirty

forty

Can you spot them?

yes	是	shi
no	不是	bushi
hello, how are you?	你好	nihao
left	左	zuo
right	右	you
thank you	谢谢	xiexie
today	今天	jintian
tomorrow	明天	mingtian
goodbye	再见	zaijian

The sounds of Mandarin Chinese by the Pinyin system, officially adopted in 1979

Words can be read almost as in English except:

Consonants:

c	as in cats
q	as in cheek
x	as in she
z	as in zero
zh	as in jar

Vowels:

a	as in far
e	as in her
i	as in tree
o	between law and roll
u	as in too
ai	as in why
ao	as in cow
ei	as in grey
ou	as in low
ui	like way

Other double vowels contain the two sounds.

Each vowel or vowel group also has four tones of voice in which it can be pronounced. These can be indicated by tone marks. Words with the same vowel but different tones have completely different meanings.

Chinese magic squares

Numbers have often been thought to have mystical properties, and particular arrangements of numbers to have special powers. The arithmetical properties of magic squares have, by now, been studied exhaustively, but in antiquity they were probably more valued as charms or for divination.

Writing in 1892, Rouse Ball tells that after magic squares became known in Europe, a silver plate engraved with a magic square was sometimes prescribed as a charm against the plague. He also notes that large passenger ships generally have one on deck for scoring such games as shuffleboard!

There are legends in China about their origin. Emperor Yu the Great, controller of the rivers, is supposed to have been given two figures by miraculous animals rising out of the waters. A turtle came out of the River Lo to give him the red Lo Shu diagram. A dragon-horse from the Yellow River gave him the green Ho Thu diagram.

• See what you can make of these diagrams:

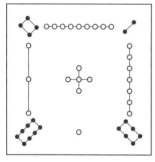

Lo Shu

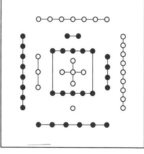

Ho Thu

In Chinese thought the Yin and the Yang are complementary life forces. You will notice that the even, or Yin, numbers are shown by black spots. The odd, or Yang, numbers are shown by white spots. The Lo Shu diagram turns out to be the now well-known magic square containing the numbers one to nine. They are arranged so that each row, column and diagonal sums to the same total of 15.

The properties of the Ho Thu are less obvious, though you will probably find some patterns and connections. It makes most sense in the light of symbolic links which were made between numbers, elements, seasons, etc. Wood, fire, metal and water relate to spring, summer, autumn and winter and to the numbers 8, 7, 9, 6. Earth at the centre is number 5. Some early Chinese writing, which has a similar tone to the magical secrets of the Pythagoreans, says:

7 × 9 makes 63. 3 governs the Great Bear. This constellation governs the dog. Therefore the dog is born after only 3 months. ...

2 × 9 makes 18. 8 governs the wind. The wind governs the insects, etc.

Later, interest focused on the number relationships themselves, rather than links with the occult. Chinese writers devised 4 by 4 magic squares (of which we now know there are 880) and higher orders. They constructed other 'magic' figures such as a wheel and a cube. By trial and error this is very tedious, but reasoning does help.

• You could try to fill a wheel in such a way that the totals along each spoke are the same and the totals around each circle are the same.

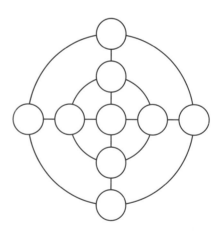

The four-spoke wheel requires nine consecutive numbers. Guesswork may suggest a solution, but in fact there are three possibilities. Find the total of the digits from 1 to 9. If these are fitted onto four spokes, what could be left over to go in the centre? What pairs are possible for the spokes? How can these be arranged to give equal totals around the circles?

• Can you extend the reasoning to an eight-spoke wheel?

A taste of Euclid

Briefing

Dip into number theory, sieving for primes, and follow Euclid's argument that they are infinite. To experience the rational emphasis of Greek mathematics, find and justify rules about odd and even numbers. Perfect numbers and a theorem about them are mentioned briefly.

Background

The Greek-speaking peoples around the Eastern Mediterranean were heirs to ancient knowledge, although exactly how much they learned, and where and when, is difficult to determine. As an indication of their burgeoning culture, the Games at Olympia are first reliably recorded in 776 BC.

The region of ancient Greece.

What we 'know' of the early mathematicians comes from traditional stories rather than hard evidence. Thales (normally pronounced Thay-lees) of the Ionian city of Miletus is generally considered to be the father of Greek mathematics. In his youth a successful merchant, he no doubt learned much through his contacts and travels. In later life he established a school to which, it is said, the young Pythagoras came. Thales is reputed to have launched the idea of deductive proof in geometry. He is also credited with successful prediction of an eclipse of the sun, which must have been just before or just after 600 BC.

Pythagoras was more of a mystic. He probably travelled in the East before setting up his secret society at Crotona in the heel of Italy about 500 BC. Theirs was an oral tradition, so we have to rely on reports by very much later writers.

There is more certainty about the Athens of Socrates, Plato and Aristotle (about 470 to 322 BC). Greek mathematics had by then developed in an original style. A sharp distinction was made between higher mathematics and the facts and computational skills used in everyday business. The philosophers were particularly interested in establishing knowledge by rational argument.

Euclid's *Elements* (*c.* 300 BC) was in a sense the culmination of this classical period. It brought together what was known of geometry (except conics) and the theory of numbers (their properties rather than computation). Everything was systematically arranged in thirteen books and established by logic. Little is known of Euclid's life, except that he taught at Alexandria and wrote this phenomenally successful textbook. Parts of it were in regular school use right until the beginning of the twentieth century!

After the empire-building of Alexander the Great, the Macedonian (356–323 BC), the focus of Greek culture shifted from Athens to Alexandria, where the great Library and Museum were established. Archimedes,[1] Eratosthenes, and Apollonius are well remembered from this time. The Roman Empire was rising, and of course Greek culture continued to flourish within it for many centuries. In the latter part of this Hellenistic Period (roughly 300 BC to AD 300), Claudius Ptolemy wrote his major work on mathematical astronomy and Diophantus his *Arithmetic*. Thereafter most writing took the form of commentary. Hypatia, the first named woman in mathematics history, lectured at Alexandria, and met a violent death there soon after AD 400.

Greek mathematics has been very thoroughly studied, but to establish a definitive history is painstaking work because of the lack of original sources. Considering that the Library of Alexandria once contained literally hundreds of thousands of papyrus rolls, this is a real tragedy. Those books which survived the turmoil presumably decayed in a moister climate than that of Upper Egypt. A few translations and copies were preserved into medieval Europe. Fortunately, Greek work was cherished in Byzantium and energetically developed in the Islamic world.

In the classroom

Pupils can get a sense of the distinctiveness of classical Greek mathematics without labouring through too many

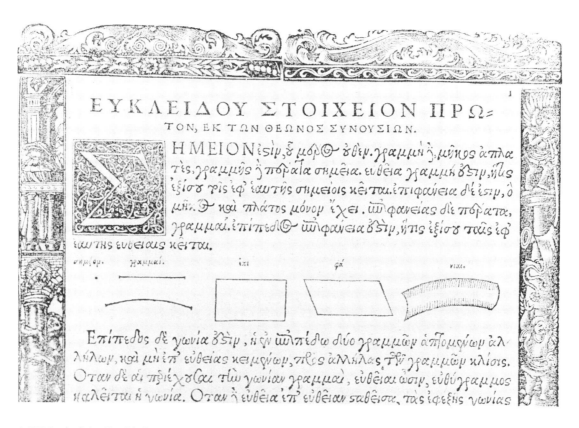

A 1533 Greek edition. The title line says it is Euclid's *Elements*; then follow definitions of point, line and surface ...

theorems. The important thing to keep in mind is that Euclid was not writing down facts for the ignorant, although his books did get used as a primer. His style of work is more realistic for those, already familiar with the facts, who are interested in the question, 'How, rationally, can we know that they are true?' It is an important step in pupils' own mathematical thinking when they can go beyond pattern recognition and statement of a general rule, to ask themselves, 'How can I be sure that my rule will always hold?'

Sieving for primes

The power of reason is perhaps best demonstrated where a question has no obvious answer. Prime numbers, and evens and odds, are promising areas to look at. Eratosthenes, who was librarian, poet and measurer of the earth's diameter, suggested a sieving method to isolate the prime numbers. Pupils can use his method on a 1 to 100 number square. Cross out all the multiples of 2 except 2 itself, and then all the multiples of 3 except 3. Four and its multiples will have gone. Do 5 next, and so on. You will be left with numbers which are not multiples of anything other than themselves (and 1), i.e. prime numbers. Why, incidentally, is it unnecessary to go beyond multiples of 7 when sieving for primes up to 100?

Do primes go on for ever?

Having used the sieve, pupils could look at the results decade by decade. How many primes in each row of the square? Some interesting questions arise quite naturally. Are the primes going to thin out as you count further on? Are they going to come to an end entirely?

Primes					
	from 1 to 10	2	3	5	7
	from 11 to 20	11	13	17	19
	from 21 to 30	23	29		
	from 31 to 40	31	37		
	from 41 to 50	41	43	47	
	from 51 to 60	53	59		
	from 61 to 70	61	67		
	from 71 to 80	71	73	79	
	from 81 to 90	83	89		
	from 91 to 100	97			

Allow pupils to speculate and encourage them to give reasons. If anyone chooses to look further, the results will still be inconclusive:

101   103   107   109
113
127
131   137   139
149

Some may want to enlist the computer, which could be instructive (a BASIC program is given in the notes)[2] but will not resolve the questions. The largest prime known in 1978 was found by two 18-year-olds using 350 hours of computer time.[3] Their prime number had 6533 digits, so we shall not attempt to print it! By 1992 a prime with almost thirty-five times as many digits, but concisely expressed as $2^{756839} - 1$, had been discovered, and so it goes on.

The distribution of primes has exercised many great minds. There is a prime number theorem which does imply that they tend to thin out.[4] This theorem was found jotted on a book of logarithm tables that belonged to Gauss, but a proof only became established a hundred years ago. However, by 300 BC, Euclid already knew with certainty that primes do not come to an end.[5]

Euclid's reasoning

Supposing three prime numbers are all you know. Multiply those three together and add 1. The number you get will not be divisible by any of the three primes you already know. (If you try to divide, there is bound to be a remainder of 1.) So *either* that number is prime itself, *or* it is divisible by a prime which is different from the three that you know about. Either way, you have found there is an extra prime number.

Exactly the same argument applies if you know millions of primes. Multiply them all together and add 1. Either that number is a new prime or it has a prime factor that was not on your original list. So you can go on for ever and you will never reach a final prime number.

Pupils are usually intrigued by the infinite, even if not all of them appreciate the details of this argument.

Reasoning about odds and evens

The theorem we have just worked through, number 20 in Euclid's Book 9, is followed by propositions about odd and even numbers which are quite accessible. They probably have their origins in Pythagorean mysticism. Pupils can investigate for themselves what rules exist and try to justify them.

To get started, ask how they are going to recognize an even number. Make sure everyone has a working definition of odd and even. Here are a few examples of the many rules which may emerge:

If you add together as many even numbers as you like, the total is even.

If you subtract an odd number from an even number ...

If you multiply an odd number by an odd number ...

and perhaps more rarely considered:

If an odd number divides exactly into an even number, it will also divide exactly into half of it.

You will have to decide what level of reasoning is acceptable. The central question is, 'How can you be sure?' Where everyone feels 'It's obvious', there is little more to be said, but where some genuine doubt exists in the minds of some pupils, others can be pushed to explain the reasons why.

At the risk of an expensive session, you might want to repeat a legend told of Euclid. One of his pupils, having learned his first theorem, enquired, 'But what shall I get by learning these things?' The master called for his slave and said, 'Give him threepence since he wants to make something out of what he learns!'

The purpose, so far as Book 9 is concerned, is to prepare the arena for an impressive theorem about perfect numbers.[6] Six is *perfect* because it is equal to the sum of its factors, $1 + 2 + 3$; similarly $28 = 1 + 2 + 4 + 7 + 14$. To express Euclid's theorem concisely, it is convenient to use algebra:

Let $S_n = 1 + 2 + 2^2 + 2^3 + \ldots + 2^{n-1}$

He shows that if S_n is prime, then $S_n \times 2^{n-1}$ will be perfect! Try it out for a few small values of n and you may begin to see why the theorem works.

Before Pythagoras – and after

Briefing

The theorem was known in ancient Babylon before Pythagoras and, most likely, before Pythagoras in India and China too. Explore the different contexts: duties of a Hindu priest, piling-up of rectangles, Chinese log and vine problems. Interpret the Babylonian tablet Plimpton 322, and investigate extensions found in Euclid's *Elements*.

Background

Pythagoras' theorem has both a spatial and a numerical aspect. Spatially it is about the area of two different squares combined to make a single square. Numerically it is about sets of three numbers which can represent the lengths of sides of a right-angled triangle. Attention naturally focuses on whole number lengths such as 3,4,5, then 5,12,13, and so on, which are generally known as Pythagorean triads or triplets. It is possible to study these triplets without connecting them to a triangle: 'Find two numbers so that, when you square each and add, the result is another square number.' This is number theory rather than Pythagoras' theorem.

However, Pythagoras was certainly not the originator of 'his' theorem! It was used on Babylonian clay tablets more than a thousand years before he lived.[1] It is more appropriate to call it the right-angled-triangle theorem, or, as explained later, the gnomon theorem.

Let us now look at the transcription of the tablet Plimpton 322 from **sheet 1.2a.** Its contents are given in the table; the first column labelled A is sexagesimal and the others are worked out in decimal. You may like to experiment, in order to establish some connections or rationale for the numbers, before reading on.

The textual headings to the columns offer a slight hint. At the top of B it says '(something unintelligible) ... of the front', and at the top of column C it says the same unintelligible word '... of the diagonal'. It seems likely that the scribe made occasional errors in such a page of work, so do not be put off by the odd contradiction to your emerging theory!

Leaving this aside for a while so as not to spoil your fun, let us look at the evidence in two other cultures for very early knowledge of the gnomon theorem.

Typical humped bull of India, made by impression with a seal from Mohenjo-Daro.

In the 1920s, archaeological excavations in the valley of the River Indus began to uncover remains of cities dating back to about 2500 BC. Two large and very similar cities are Mohenjo-Daro and Harappa (in the Punjab region). Then came further sites in the Ganges Valley and a large city at Lothal (in modern Gujarat), indicating a wide spreading of the Harappan civilization. From the west coast, a flourishing trade was carried on with ancient Babylon. Merchants used stone seals to imprint their trademark on clay tags, but their pictographic script has not been deciphered. Two features of this sophisticated society stand out: indoor plumbing and the firing of bricks. The bricks, of standard dimensions and

A		B	C	D
	15	119	169	1
	58/14/50/6/15	3367	11521	2
	1/15/33/45	4601	6649	3
5	29/32/52/16	12709	18541	4
48/54/	1/40	65	97	
47/	6/41/40	319	481	
43/11/56/28/26/40		2291	3541	7
41/33/59/ 3/45		799	1249	8
38/33/36/36		541	769	9
35/10/2/28/27/24/26/40		4961	8161	10
33/45	45	75	11	
29/24/54/ 2/15		1679	2929	12
27/ 3/45 25921		289	13	
25/48/51/35/6/40		1771	3229	
23/13/46/40		56	53	

excellent quality, were used for embankments against the floods and for building municipal granaries. This technology came to influence the succeeding culture in a surprising way.

Around 1800 BC, the Harappan cities abruptly declined. A different people, described as Aryans, came in from the north and by 1500 BC Hindu civilization was emerging. With it came the Sanskrit language, the Vedas and the Upanishads. The Vedas contain hymns and so forth for ceremonial occasions, but, in appendices known as Sulbasutras, there are detailed instructions for the laying-out of sacrificial altars. These were intricate, and designed to be built out of bricks of specific shapes and sizes! The cord used for measuring out the ground came to be known as a *sulba*.

Dating is hazy. What may have first been written in 500 BC may have been known hundreds of years earlier. The sutras are expressed in condensed form so as to be easily memorized and passed on orally. For our purpose, the contents are important for what they reveal of a mathematical tradition, in particular the prominence of the gnomon theorem.[2] For instance, ritual required that when a sequence of altars was built they should increase in size but maintain the same shape: 'Given a square of $7\frac{1}{2}$ square purushas, how to increase it to $8\frac{1}{2}$ square purushas? For an answer, draw a rectangle having one side equal to that of the $7\frac{1}{2}$ square and the other of length 1 purusha. The diagonal of this rectangle gives the correct length for the side of the required square.'

In China, in the astronomical work *Zhoubi suanjing*, we meet the *gougu* theorem. This term arises from the naming of the sides. Not only does the hypotenuse have a name, *xian*, meaning the string of a bow, but the short side is called *gou* (width or leg) and the other side *gu* (length or thigh).[3]

A leg and thigh bend into an L-shape. An L-shaped instrument known as a gnomon was carried by Chinese astronomers/surveyors. The word 'gnomon' refers generally to L-shapes: a carpenter's square, a stake and its shadow, the pin of a sundial and so on. The shadow gnomon was used to get an estimate of the sun's distance.[4]

There are more problems in the ninth chapter of the *Jiuzhang suanshu*. Some, for which we should use quadratic equations, are solved there by geometrical methods. Whether or not this preceded Pythagoras is debatable, but let us return to the Babylonian tablet which certainly did.

In each row in the table on page 24 you can take the number in column C to be the hypotenuse and the one in column B to be the *gu*. Each time $\sqrt{(C^2 - B^2)}$, which is the length of the *gou*, turns out to be a whole number, except of course for the scribe's mistakes. You may now be able

to mark his work (unlikely to be her work) showing corrections – only four thousand years late!

But why are such a mixture of large and small numbers used in such a peculiar order? You may have found a clue by looking at the ratios of column B to column C:

119/169	= 0.704
3367/11521 (a scribal error here?)	= 0.292
4601/6649	= 0.691
12709/18541	= 0.685
65/79	= 0.670
319/481	= 0.663
2291/3541	= 0.647
799/1249	= 0.640

etc.

There is a sequence here which we should call the sine of the angle. The triplets might have been discovered and arranged so that the angle changed by a sequence of small amounts from 45° to 32°. Something of the sort seems to be happening in column A. The numbers here are the result of calculating $B^2/(C^2 - B^2)$, the equivalent of $\tan^2$, an odd quantity to require. Various alternative explanations have been proposed,[5] but despite doubts over details it seems certain that the Babylonians had an efficient method for generating Pythagorean triplets. Alone, this could have been an exercise in number theory, but the evidence of other tablets[6] confirms that such triplets were related to right-angled triangles.

So what was the Greek contribution? **Sheet 5.4** contains two appreciations. The ox story is dubious, but Euclid does indeed generalize the theorem to any type of figure on the sides of a right-angled triangle.[7]

Hobbes is a nice example of those who have been thrilled by Euclid's proof of the basic theorem (which is rather lengthy for inclusion here). In the context of proof, you might like to consider the piling-up of rectangles on sheet 5.2. As it stands, this seems to demonstrate only a particular case, but it generalizes in a most straightforward way.

In the classroom

The oldest source is not the easiest. Suitable starting points for introducing pupils to the theorem are given on **sheet 5.1** or **sheet 5.2**. Any of the four sheets may be used for consolidation and extension work with pupils who have already met the theorem.

A brahman priest asks a question about squares

Rather than starting with sheet 5.1, try posing the fundamental problem: how to combine two squares to make one square of the same total area. For two equal squares, pupils can easily discover a method, using a pair of scissors for instance:

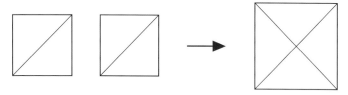

Two equal squares merged to one.

After success with this, they can investigate the more general case with geoboards or by drawing on dotty paper:

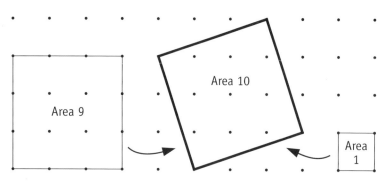

Two unequal squares merged to one.

Sheet 5.1 illustrates the rule given in the Sulbasutras. The heading is in devanagari script, developed for writing Sanskrit and still in use today. It reads, 'Sulbasutras of Baudhayana and Apastamba'.

Sheet 5.1 (part 2) applies Pythagorean triplets to the practical task of marking out the sacred ground, or *vedi*.[8] Simulate this by drawing, with thin cord and drawing pins in place of posts, or out of doors with rope. Outdoors shows it more realistically of course, because it is apparent that an ordinary set-square is useless for such large-scale work. The shape required is an isosceles trapezium. Draw a sketch diagram for your chosen method, such as one of those below.

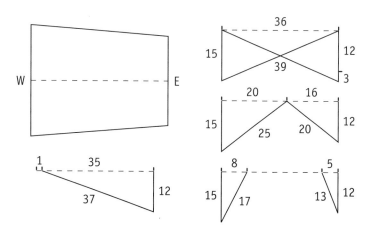

Start marking out with the east–west line or *prachi* measuring 36 units. It is worth using several of the methods on the same diagram in order to check the placing of the corners. Then list each of the Pythagorean triplets which occur and/or invent more methods!

Alternative introduction in Chinese legend

The snippets of the conversation on **sheet 5.2** give a hint of both mystical and practical connotations.

Pupils should read the first section and reconstruct the diagram step by step. For a more interesting challenge, they can produce similar diagrams with different dimensions. Then they could write a revised commentary, for instance:

> *Make a rectangle 5 by 12. Draw a square on its diagonal, and surround it by triangles like that which has been left outside, so as to form a square plate. Thus the four triangles make an area of 120. When this is subtracted from the square plate (of area 17×17) the remainder is 169. This is the area of the square on the diagonal (which must have a side of length 13).*

More advanced pupils may be able to generalize to an *x* by *y* rectangle.

The second section of conversation is about uses of the right-angled triangle or gnomon, not particularly connected to the theorem. Pupils can illustrate and describe some of these uses in their own words. Some of the uses appear again in a practical context in chapter 8.

Consolidation and extension

Sheet 5.3: problems using the *gougu* theorem. These are amongst the simpler ones from the ninth chapter of the *Jiuzhang suanshu*. However, they are not routine: imagination, reasoning and maybe algebra are required.

Sheet 1.2a: investigate this amazing collection of Pythagorean triplets as suggested in the background.

Sheet 5.4: extensions in Euclid, for discussion, and to prompt investigation of the more general theorem.

बोधयाना एव आपस्तम्बा के सुल्बसूत्र

To merge two squares to obtain a third square:

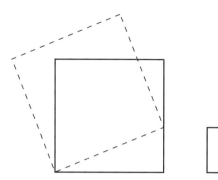

To lay out the Mahavedi

The middle line, running east–west, is 36 feet long. Fix a pole at each end of the line.

To the cord of length 36 feet, add 18 feet. Make two marks on the cord at 12 and at 15 feet, starting from the western end. Tie the ends of the cord to the posts. Taking the cord by the mark at 15, take it towards the south.

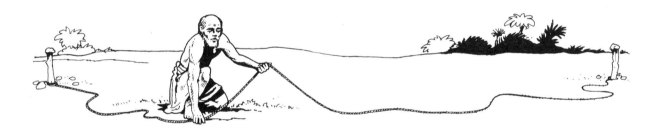

When the cord is tightly stretched, fix a pole. Do the same on the northern side.

After that, exchange the ends of the cord. Take it by the mark 15 again and stretch it southwards, but this time put in the pole at the mark of 12 feet. Do the same on the north side. This is the measurement of the *vedi* by means of one cord.

Another way

Fix a pole on the E–W line at P, 16 feet from E. Tie a cord of 32 feet length to this pole and to the one at E. Mark the cord at 12 feet from E and draw this point towards the south. Place a post when the cord becomes taut. Do the same on the north side.

Now with a cord of 40 feet tied at P and at W, and marked at 15 feet from W, mark out the south-west and north-west corners of the *vedi*.

Two other ways of marking the eastern corners

Fix a pole 5 feet from E. Use a cord of 25 feet length with a mark at 12 feet.

Fix a pole 35 feet from E. Use a cord of 49 feet length with a mark at 12 feet.

Another way of marking the western corners

Fix a pole 8 feet from W. Use a cord of 32 feet length with a mark at 15 feet.

The Gnomon and the Circular Paths of Heaven

Of old, Zhōu Gōng addressed Shāng Gāo,
   'I should like to ask you, what was the origin of these numbers?'

   Shāng Gāo replied ...

'... let us cut a rectangle, and make the width 3, and the length 4. The diagonal between the two corners will then be 5 units long. Now draw a square on this diagonal. Then surround it with half-rectangles like that which has been left outside, so as to form a square plate.

'The four outer half-rectangles together make two rectangles (of total area 24). The area of the square plate is 49. Taking off the outer half-rectangles, the remainder is of area 25.

'This process is called "piling up the rectangles". The methods used by Yu the Great in governing the world were derived from these numbers.'

Zhōu Gōng exclaimed,	'Great indeed is the art of numbering. I would like to ask about the Tao of the use of the right-angled triangle.'
Shāng Gāo replied,	'The plane right-angled triangle laid on the ground serves to lay out straight and square by the aid of cords.

The recumbent right-angled triangle serves to observe heights.
The reverse right-angled triangle serves to fathom depths.
The flat right-angled triangle is used for finding distances.
By rotating the right-angled triangle a circle may be formed.
By uniting right-angled triangles squares and rectangles are formed.

'The square pertains to earth, the circle belongs to heaven ... Heaven is like a conical sun-hat. Heaven's colours are blue and black, earth's colours are yellow and red ... He who understands the earth is a wise man, and he who understands the heavens is a sage ... and the combination of the right angle with numbers is what guides and rules the ten thousand things.'

Zhōu Gōng exclaimed,   'Excellent indeed.'

Jiǔzhāng suànshù, chapter nine

The gōugǔ theorem (pronounced go-goo):

$$\text{gōu}^2 + \text{gǔ}^2 = \text{xián}^2$$

gōu can also mean 'leg or width'.
gǔ can also mean 'thigh or length'.
xián can also mean 'bow string'.

(4)

Given: A wooden log of diameter 2 chǐ 5 cùn. A plank is to be cut from the log. If the plank is 7 cùn thick, how broad can it be?

Answer: 2 chǐ 4 cùn.

- Draw the circular cross-section of a log, and show how the end of the plank fits in.
- How many cùn (Chinese inch) could there be to a chǐ (Chinese foot)?

(6)

Given: In the centre of a square pond whose side is 10 chǐ there grows a reed whose top reaches 1 chǐ above the water level. If we pull the reed over to the bank, its top is level with the water's surface. What is the depth of the pond and the length of the plant?

Answer: The depth of water is 12 chǐ and the length of the plant is 13 chǐ.

Method: Find the square of half the pond's width, and from it subtract the square of 1 chǐ. The depth of the water will be equal to the difference divided by twice the height of the reed above the water (1 chǐ). To find the length of the plant we add 1 chǐ to the result.

- Write your own explanation for this one.

(5)

Given: A tree of height 20 chǐ has a circumference of 3 chǐ. There is an arrow-root vine which winds seven times around the tree and reaches to the top. What is the length of the vine?

Answer: 29 chǐ.

Methods: The gǔ equals 7 times 3 chǐ, that is 21 chǐ. Gōu equals the height of the tree, that is 20 chǐ. The length of the vine is equal to the xián.

Explanation: One can understand the problem by winding a string around a writing brush. When unwound ...

- Try to picture the problem and draw a diagram to show why the length of the vine is xián.

(13)

Given: A bamboo shoot 10 chǐ tall breaks so that the main shoot and the broken portion form a triangle. The top touches the ground 3 chǐ from the stem. What is the length of the stem left standing upright?

Answer: $4\frac{11}{20}$ chǐ.

- Try to find your own method of solving this.
- List the 'Pythagorean triplets' which occur in these four problems.

Gnomon theorem in Euclid's *Elements*

Proclus, who taught in Athens during the fifth century AD, produced a commentary on the first book of Euclid. His hint of scepticism about the Pythagoras legend is shared by modern scholars. Remember that even Proclus was writing 1000 years after Pythagoras lived. He has this to say about proposition 47:

... If we listen to those who like to record antiquities, we shall find some of them attributing this theorem to Pythagoras and saying that he sacrificed an ox on its discovery. For my part, though I marvel at those who first noted the truth of this theorem, I admire the author of the Elements, not only for the very lucid proof by which he made it fast, but because he compelled assent to the still more general theorem by the irrefutable arguments of science in the sixth book. For in that book [prop. 31] he proves generally that, in right-angled triangles, the figure on the hypotenuse is equal to mathematically similar figures described on the other two sides.

... the cause of the more general proposition that is proved becomes clear: it is the rightness of the angle that makes the figure on the hypotenuse equal to the similar and similarly drawn figures on the containing sides, just as the obtuseness of the angle is the cause of its being greater and the acuteness of the angle the cause of its being less.

Further admiration for the proof of the basic theorem came from Thomas Hobbes, of whom John Aubrey writes:

The day of his Birth was April the fifth, Anno Domini 1588, on a Fryday morning, which that yeare was Good Fryday. His mother fell in labour with him upon the fright of the Invasion of the Spaniards ...

At fower yeer old Mr Thomas Hobbes (Philosopher) went to Schoole in Westport church till 8 – then the church was painted. At 8 he could read well and number a matter of 4 or 5 figures ...

He was 40 yeares old before he looked on Geometry; which happened accidentally. Being in a Gentleman's Library, Euclid's Elements lay open, and 'twas the 47 prop. ... He read the Proposition. By G—, sayd he (he would now and then sweare an emphaticall Oath by way of emphasis) this is impossible! So he reads the demonstration of it, which referred him back to such a Proposition; which proposition he read. That referred him back to another, which he also read. *Et sic deinceps* [and so on] until at last he was demonstratively convinced of that trueth. This made him in love with Geometry.

... I have heard Mr Hobbes say that he was wont to draw lines on his thigh and on the sheetes, abed, and also to multiply and divide.

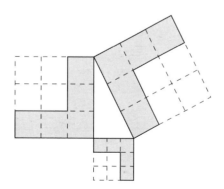

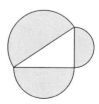

Mathematically similar figures on each side of a right-angled triangle

Numbering the sand

Briefing

This is one to tickle the imagination, best for younger pupils who can still admit to enjoying a fantasy, though there is material for any age.

Read and write numbers greater than a thousand, and do calculations with them. Relate units of measurement. Explore the very large (or small) in imagination or in science.

Background

The Sand Reckoner[1] is unique amongst Greek mathematical works. It was written during the third century BC by the unique character, Archimedes.

By contrast, Indian mathematics had a traditional fascination with large numbers. In one legend[2] it is told how, in order to win his bride, Buddha was challenged to name all the numbers above one hundred kotis (that is, above ten million). This is the beginning of Buddha's naming[3] of the numbers:

ayuta	1 000 000 000	(100 kotis)
niyuta	100 000 000 000	(100 ayutas)
kangkara	10 000 000 000 000	
vivara	1 000 000 000 000 000	

Notice that each increase is a hundredfold. The naming continues:

aksobhya

vivaha

utsanga

bahula

nagabala

titilambha

vyavasthanapradjnapti

hetuhila

until the twenty-third in sequence:

tallaksana.

This is 10^{53} in index notation and yet completes only the first stage of counting. The rhythm goes upwards in sequences of twenty-three. The numbers are leaping beyond imagination, but they are given names, and with names the mind has at least some grip.

Capability with large numbers was not restricted to the Buddhist tradition. By the time of Archimedes, Jainist mathematicians[4] had developed a classification of numbers which began with three groups: countable, innumerable, and infinite. Jainism, like Hinduism from which it sprang, takes a special interest in long stretches of time and space. This is illustrated in one of the early writings, the *Anuyoga Dwara Sutra*:

Consider a trough whose diameter is that of the Earth. Fill it up with white mustard seeds, counting one after another. Similarly fill up with mustard seeds other troughs of the sizes of the various lands and seas. Still the highest countable number has not been reached.[5]

The parallel between these examples from the Indian continent and the Greek *Sand Reckoner* is remarkable, but the styles are different. Since Archimedes lived in a seaside town, it is not surprising that his imagination touched on sand, whereas in the midst of a huge continent the Jains counted mustard seeds. But Archimedes was not concerned with coining new number names; he was content to use the Greek 'myriad' as a building block. His aim was to set an upper bound for the number of grains of sand which could fill the known universe. He approached this using his tried method of setting limits and by applying estimation to the measurements. Before looking at details, here is a biographical sketch.

ARCHIMEDES lived at the time when Greek dominance in the Mediterranean was beginning to give way to an expanding Roman Empire. Greek learning still flourished, centred at Alexandria with its renowned Museum and Library. The books of course were written on scrolls of papyrus; by Archimedes' time the catalogue alone filled 120 of these rolls. Archimedes himself lived at Syracuse on the island of Sicily. He may have visited the community of scholars at Alexandria; he certainly wrote letters to several of them, including Eratosthenes the librarian.

Archimedes stands out as a master of classical geometric logic but also as a practical genius. The 'Eureka' story[6] is well known; he also wrote on areas, volumes, curves, the principle of levers and centres of gravity. Legend has it that he demonstrated how one man could pull a loaded ship from the water with ropes and a pulley system.[7] When the Romans attacked Syracuse he is purported to have burned their ships in the harbour by focusing sunlight with curved mirrors. The catapults and other machines he devised caused havoc among the enemy troops. When the city was eventually taken after a two-year siege, a soldier is said to have come upon Archimedes absorbed in a mathematical problem! The soldier grew impatient with the old man and slew him.[8] According to one account, this happened when Archimedes was 75 years old. Syracuse fell in 212 BC, so Archimedes was probably born in 287 BC.

So now (in paraphrase) the opening text of his *Sand Reckoner*:

> *There are some, King Gelon, who think that the grains of sand on the shore are infinitely many. I mean by the sand not only what there is around Syracuse and the rest of Sicily, but all the sand in every place, whether inhabited or uninhabited.*

> *Again there are some who don't think it is infinite but still believe that no number has been named which is great enough to match it. If these people imagined the whole earth made of sand, with all the seas and hollows filled up to the height of the highest mountains, they would be even further from thinking of a number to express the amount.*

> *But I will try to show you that I can name such a number.*

> *More than that, I have named a number greater than the grains of sand which would fill the whole universe![9]*

To achieve this feat, Archimedes had to estimate the size of the earth and of the universe. He also had to invent some very large numbers. There were two theories about the universe from which to choose. The popular idea was that sun, moon and stars revolved around the earth, but Aristarchus had come up with the notion that the earth revolved around the sun and that out beyond was a fixed sphere of stars which formed the edge of the universe. Without necessarily accepting the theory, Archimedes naturally rose to the challenge of filling this larger universe with sand!

His approach was not so much to count the sand, as to set an upper limit on the number of grains there could possibly be. This is such an important strategy in estimation work that it is worth illustrating one facet of his argument.

First he surmised the diameter of the sun. Then he took his own measurements of the angle which it subtends at the earth (not to be attempted by pupils because of the risk to eyesight). From this he could tell that about 800 sun-widths would encompass the 'popular' universe, so a thousand sun-widths would certainly be more than enough. Thus, in order to establish an upper bound for the size, he based his calculation on a chiliagon (polygon with 1000 sides). Further suppositions enabled him to scale up this 'popular' universe to the universe of Aristarchus.

The highest named number of the Greeks was a 'myriad', in our terms ten thousand. So Archimedes pointed out:

> *Therefore we can express numbers up to a myriad myriads. Let these be called numbers of the first order.*

His simple but powerful idea was then to take a myriad myriads as the unit for a second order of numbers. This took him to a myriad-myriad myriad-myriads or 10^{16}. Unstoppable then to the myriad-myriadth order, he had achieved numbers up to what for us would be 1 followed by 800 000 000 zeros. He went much further, but this is already more than sufficient for the sand-reckoning. Giving Archimedes the last word:

> *Take a quantity of sand not greater than a poppy-seed and suppose that it contains no more than a myriad grains. Next suppose the diameter of the poppy-seed to be at least $\frac{1}{40}$ of a finger-breadth …*

> *From this we can prove that the number of grains in*

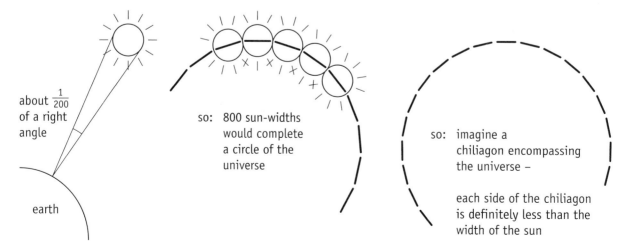

about $\frac{1}{200}$ of a right angle

earth

so: 800 sun-widths would complete a circle of the universe

so: imagine a chiliagon encompassing the universe –

each side of the chiliagon is definitely less than the width of the sun

Estimating the 'popular' universe.

Aristarchus' sphere of the fixed stars would be less than 10 000 000 units of the eighth order of numbers. [A mere 10^{63}.] I know that these things, King Gelon, will appear incredible to the great majority of people who have not studied mathematics, but I thought the subject would be appropriate for you.

In the classroom

The background will be helpful in suggesting lines of development and in answering questions which may arise, but to start with, pupils will become more involved if they can do their own thing. Trying to follow the reasoning of the ancients comes later.

A story to start off with

Two hundred years before Julius Caesar came to Britain, there was a man living on the island of Sicily whose name was Ἀρχιμήδης. He wrote a letter to the king, and this is what he said …

The introductory paragraph of the extract from Archimedes could then be read:

There are some, King Gelon, who think that the grains of sand on the shore are infinitely many. I mean by the sand not only what there is around Syracuse and the rest of Sicily, but all the sand in every place, whether inhabited or uninhabited.

Again there are some who don't think it is infinite but still believe that no number has been named which is great enough to match it. If these people imagined the whole earth made of sand, with all the seas and hollows filled up to the height of the highest mountains, they would be even further from thinking of a number to express the amount.

But I will try to show you that I can name such a number.

More than that, I have named a number greater than the grains of sand which would fill the whole universe![9]

This leads naturally to questions such as:

What large numbers do you know?

How would you write them?

Make a table to show the pattern:

a million	1 000 000	
a billion	1 000 000 000 000	a million-million
a trillion	1 000 000 000 000 000 000	a million-billion
a quadrillion …		a million-trillion
a quintillion …		a million-million-million-million-million

This is the British table; in the USA a billion is a thousand million and a trillion is a thousand billion (in other words, a US trillion is a British billion). The US table is:

a million	1 000 000	
a billion	1 000 000 000	a thousand-million
a trillion	1 000 000 000 000	a million-million
a quadrillion …		a thousand-million-million

American usage is often adopted in Britain, especially for money; thus £1 000 000 000 is a billion pounds on both sides of the Atlantic. A googol is a fanciful name (not in formal use) for 10^{100} and a googolplex is 10^{googol}.

For units of measurement, terms have been internationally defined (SI units):

10^3	kilo-	10^{12}	tera-
10^6	mega-	10^{15}	peta-
10^9	giga-	10^{18}	exa-

Thus the mass of the earth is about six thousand million exagrams (6×10^{27} g).

There is a corresponding series going downwards:

10^{-3}	milli-	10^{-12}	pico-
10^{-6}	micro-	10^{-15}	femto-
10^{-9}	nano-	10^{-18}	atto-

The mass of a single carbon atom is about 20 millionths of an attogram (2×10^{-23} g).

Follow-on possibilities

1 *Practise writing down large numbers given the words, and saying numbers given the symbols. For instance:*

The Hubble telescope repair cost $630 million.[10]
Write $630 000 000.

The sun is 93 000 000 miles away.
Say 'ninety-three million miles'.

How many centimetre cubes to a metre cube?

2 *Pupils suggest questions with large number answers.* For instance:

> How many breakfasts have you eaten in your life?

> Alpha Centauri is 4.35 light years away. How many miles is that, given that light travels 186000 miles in a second?

Tackle the calculations. Either estimate mentally by single digit arithmetic: for example,

> 186000 miles per sec
> approximately $200000 \times 60 \times 60$ mph
> gives approximately 700000000 mph;

or use a calculator. This will give a gentle introduction to standard index form, since answers come up in such formats as 2.55158E+13 (the answer to the Alpha Centauri question).

3 *How many grains of rice to fill this box?* Build up to an estimate, Archimedes style. How many grains to a matchbox? How many matchboxes to a shoebox? etc. Fix the upper limit, saying 'You could certainly not get more than ____ grains in the box.'

How many centimetre cubes to a cubic metre? This works well when done practically. Make a square metre out of centimetre squared paper. Then start to spread centimetre cubes over it. Reckon that 10000 (a myriad) would cover it to a depth of 1cm. A hundred of these layers would fill a cubic metre. The answer is a million.

4 *Invent your own large units.* Jains led the way in time measurement:[11]

The wheel of time rotates eternally. It has twelve spokes, six ascending for the time of progress and six descending for the time of deterioration. A complete turn takes one kalpa or 20×10^{14} years.

A palya is the time it will take to empty a cubic vessel of side 1 yojanna (10km) filled with the wool of new-born lambs if one strand is removed every century!

How does the age of the earth, which we now think to be some 4000 million years, compare with a kalpa or a palya?

Granaries, dykes and pyramids

Briefing

Basic work on the volume of prisms and pyramids is set in the context of ancient China and Egypt.

Trapezia occur as bases of the prisms; practise finding their areas. Work on some alternative approaches to approximating the volume of a cylinder and the area of a circle.

Find the volume of pyramids and truncated pyramids. Follow reasoning about dissections. Extend by designing and making solid models in cardboard (or wood). Investigate ways of combining them.

Background

Background to ancient Egypt and China is given in chapters 2 and 3.

In the classroom

Sheet 7.1 Area; Sheet 7.2 Volume

The problems have been adapted from the *Jiuzhang suanshu, Nine Chapters on the Mathematical Art*.[1] They are routine questions requiring areas of rectangles, triangles and trapezia and volumes of trapezoidal prisms. Set in the context of wall building and ditch digging, the later questions involve calculation of the workforce required.

Sheet 7.3 Volume of pyramids

Problems on the square-based pyramids of ancient Egypt can be tackled by the standard formula:

Volume = $\frac{1}{3}$ base area × height

Pupils should apply common sense to problem 3 about the truncated pyramid, sometimes called a frustum of a pyramid. Presumably they will subtract the volume of the top, smaller pyramid from the volume of the whole to give the volume of the base, a partially built pyramid.

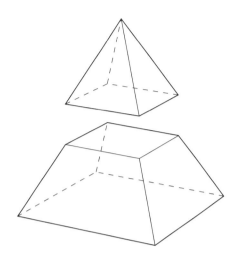

It is possible to find the base volume directly: a method is given in one problem on the Moscow papyrus.[2] The scribe demonstrates how to find the volume of a truncated pyramid, given only the dimensions of the square base, the square top and the height. The translation on the sheet shows the typical style of scribal instructions. Pupils can follow these and apply the method to further examples for themselves.

Writing the method as a formula, we obtain:

Volume = $(c^2 + cb + b^2)h/3$

You can probably derive this without much difficulty by algebraic manipulation, but how was it originally discovered? Speculation by historians has produced no very convincing answer, so your class, with the freshness of their young minds, might like to indulge in some speculation of their own.

Sheet 7.4 Dissections and reasoning

Quite surprisingly, the same method for volume of a truncated pyramid is given in the *Jiuzhang*, where it likewise occurs without any explanation. However, Liu Hui, the famous third-century commentator, does give proof. The essence of the proof is reproduced on the sheet. It is based on dissection of the truncated pyramid. The pieces are rearranged in different ways to form rectangular blocks, leading to equivalencies from which the result is deduced. Liu Hui takes the particular case where $c = 1$, $h = 1$ and $b = 3$, but the principle can be generalized. What makes this case particularly easy to handle is the fact that the corner pieces cut off are $1 \times 1 \times 1$ skew pyramids, known as *yang ma*. These can physically be reassembled in threes to make cubical blocks.

To follow Liu's argument is a splendid exercise in visualization, but some pupils will need the help of models they can handle. Designing the nets, drawing them accurately, cutting, folding and gluing are worthwhile exercises. In order to obtain sufficient pieces, pupils can work in groups. An alternative, for those familiar with a good graphical design package, is to use the computer.

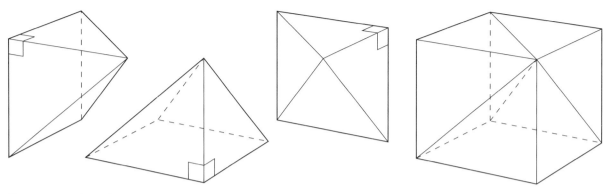

Three *yang ma* make a cube.

Whilst engaged in construction, arrange to make some of the 'turtle's shoulder joints' or *bie 'nao* which are shown on the sheet. These are halves of the *yang ma*, cut along its plane of symmetry. They are tetrahedra, but not regular ones. A possible net is shown here. All the edges marked with a small circle must be equal in length. (See notes for an alternative method of construction using wood.)[3]

A project. The *yang ma* is $\frac{1}{3}$ of a cube, the *bie 'nao* is $\frac{1}{6}$ of a cube and the wedge is $\frac{1}{2}$ of a cube. One possibility is for pupils to make composite shapes out of these, give them names and work out the volumes. Two examples, of types which occur in the *Jiuzhang*, are illustrated on the sheet.

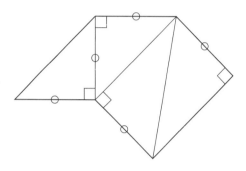

A net for the *bie 'nao*.

Sheet 7.5 Cylinders and circles

The area of a circle is also significant as the base area of a cylinder. This sheet gives an Egyptian method, from the Rhind papyrus, for the volume of a cylindrical granary, and a Chinese method, from the *Jiuzhang*, for the volume of a hill fort. They are quite different methods, and different from our own πr^2.

To appreciate the differences, pupils should make the necessary measurements on a variety of cylindrical objects (drinks can, sweets tube, large drum, etc.). For the Egyptian method you measure the diameter and the height; for the Chinese method you need measure only the circular perimeter and the height.

All the methods are approximations. In the modern method, the accuracy depends on how many significant figures of π are used in the computation. Pupils can calculate the volumes of their cylindrical objects by each method and compare results. How many significant figures of each answer are to be trusted?

The origin of the ancient methods is not known, but in the Egyptian case there is a clue, elaborated on the sheet. The area of the octagon inscribed in the square is $\frac{63}{81}$ of the square. The Egyptians actually took $\frac{64}{81}$ of (diameter)^2 for the area of the circle. Clearly if they did use the octagon, they applied a correction. The $\frac{64}{81}$ does indeed give the better approximation, but how did they know?

The Chinese $\frac{1}{12}P^2$ gives the same result as we would achieve by taking $\pi = 3$, a fairly rough approximation. Liu Hui refined this considerably, to give a ratio of circumference to diameter of $\frac{3927}{1250}$ ($= 3.1416$) and a fifth-century commentator gave $\frac{355}{113}$ which works out even more accurately (to 7 significant figures in fact).

An interesting feature of the *Jiuzhang* itself is that in a separate chapter the area of a circle is given as $\frac{1}{2}P \times \frac{1}{2}D$. This relationship is precisely true, but you need to know both the perimeter and the diameter in order to apply it. The sheet gives two dissections of the circle which pupils can do practically. Each leads directly to this same formula, but there is no evidence that either was used in ancient China.

7.1

Field measurement

禹濬畎澮圖

Discover the size of units

1 Now we have a field, 15 paces wide and 16 paces long. The question is: How big is the field? The answer is 1 mǔ.

What is the size of a mǔ?

2 There is another field, 12 paces wide and 14 paces long. The question is: How big is the field? The answer is 168 bù.

What is the size of a bù?

Yu the Great caused the channels to be dug and deepened.

Now find some areas

25 Now we have a triangular field, width 12 paces and perpendicular length 21 paces. The question is: How big is the field (in bù)?

26 Further we have a triangular field, width $5\frac{1}{2}$ paces, length $8\frac{2}{3}$ paces. The question is: How big is the field?

The rule is: Halve the width, and multiply by the perpendicular length.

27 Now we have a trapezium-like field. At one end the breadth is 30 paces, at the other end it is 42 paces. The perpendicular length is 64 paces. The question is: How big is the field (in mǔ)?

28 There is a further field, the perpendicular breadth is 65 paces, one side is of length 100 paces, the other of length 72 paces. The question is: How big is the field?

29 Now we have a field in the shape of a basket. The top width is 20 paces, the lower width is 5 paces and the perpendicular length is 30 paces. The question is: How big is the field?

30 Another field in the basket shape has an upper width of 117 paces, a lower width of 50 paces and a perpendicular length of 135 paces. The question is: How big is the field?

The rule reads: Add the parallel sides and halve the result. Then multiply by the perpendicular length or breadth. Also you can halve the perpendicular length or breadth and multiply by the sum of the parallel sides.

Construction consultations

2 Now we have a rampart. The lower width is 40 feet, the upper width is 20 feet. The height is 50 feet and the length is 1265 feet.
Question: How much is the volume (in cubic feet)?

Building a tamped earth wall

3 Now we have a wall. The lower width is 3 feet, the upper width is 2 feet, the height is 12 feet and the length $225\frac{8}{10}$ feet.
Question: How much is the volume?

4 Now we have a dam. The lower width is 20 feet, the upper width is 8 feet, the height is 4 feet, and the length is 127 feet.
Question: How much is the volume?

In the winter employment, the output per man is 444 cubic feet.
Question: How big is the workforce?

5 Now we have a water channel. The upper width is 15 feet, the lower width is 10 feet, the depth is 5 feet and the length is 70 feet.
Question: How much is the volume?

In spring work, the output per man is 766 cubic feet but they only accomplish $\frac{4}{5}$ of this.
Question: How big is the workforce?

6 Now we have a castle moat. The upper width is $16\frac{3}{10}$ feet, the lower width is 10 feet, the depth is $6\frac{3}{10}$ feet and the length is $132\frac{1}{10}$ feet.
Question: How much is the volume?

In summer work, the output per man is 871 cubic feet, but they achieve $\frac{1}{5}$ less. When $\frac{2}{3}$ of the work with sand, chalk, water and stones has already been done, how much has each man left to finish his output?

7 Now a canal has been dug. The upper width is 18 feet, the lower width is $3\frac{6}{10}$ feet, the depth is 18 feet, the length is 51 824 feet.
Question: How much is the volume?

For autumn work, the output per man is 300 cubic feet.
Question: How big is the workforce?

Pyramids of Egypt

Three Pharaohs of the Old Kingdom had pyramids built for them at Giza.
Two were remembered as tyrants, one as a kind ruler –
you can easily guess which!

Khufu: 230 metres base, 147 metres high. This is the 'great' pyramid.
Khafre: 216 metres base, 144 metres high.
Menkaure: $108\frac{1}{2}$ metres base, $66\frac{1}{2}$ metres high.

Khafre, who was Khufu's son, also had the sphinx carved in his likeness.

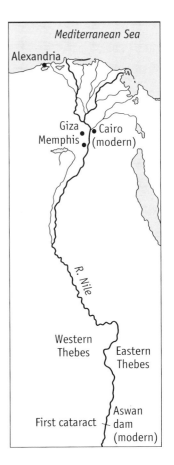

The tombs of (left to right) Menkaure, Khafre and Khufu at Giza

1 Choose one of the pyramids and find its volume.

2 Roughly how many times larger is it than your classroom?

3 Find the volume when the building work got to half its height.

4 How much volume was left to build when it reached $\frac{3}{4}$ height?

From the Moscow Mathematical Papyrus

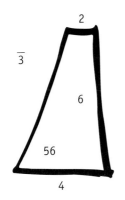

Method of calculating a truncated pyramid.

If it is put to you, a truncated pyramid of 6 cubits height, of 4 cubits base, by 2 cubits the top.

Reckon with this 4, squaring. Result 16.
Take the 2 times the 4. Result 8.
Reckon with the 2, squaring. Result 4.

Add together this 16, with this 8, with this 4. Result 28.

Calculate $\frac{1}{3}$ of the 6. Result 2.
Calculate with 28 times this 2. Result 56.

Lo! It is 56! You have found rightly.

You have correctly found it

5 Test this method by using it to do question 3 again.
Does it work correctly?

6 Show the scribe how to write a formula to sum up his method.

7 How might the method have been discovered?

Liú Huī's dissections

Try to make a mental picture of the pieces listed and to follow through the reasoning in your imagination.

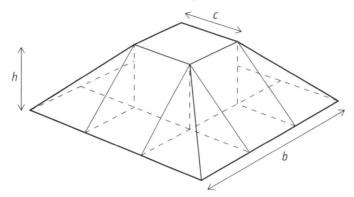

Liú Huī's dissection of a truncated pyramid

To make it easier, let the central block be a unit cube. That is what Liú Huī did. So $c = 1$, $b = 3$, $h = 1$.

The frustum can be cut up into:

> a central block measuring c by c by h
> 4 wedge shapes
> 4 corner pyramids, known as *yáng mǎ*.

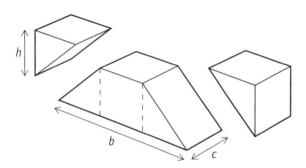

A central block with 4 wedges can be arranged to make a cuboid measuring c by b by h.

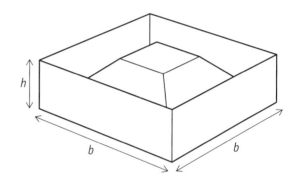

Imagine a box holding the frustum. It needs 4 more wedges and 8 *yáng mǎ* to fill it.

Add the following:	Volume
one central block	$c \times c \times h$
a central block with 4 wedges	$c \times b \times h$
the filled box	$b \times b \times h$

The total is: 3 central blocks, 12 wedges and 12 *yáng mǎ*
but this is the same total as 3 frustums.

So the volume of one frustum is $\frac{1}{3}(c \times c \times h + c \times b \times h + b \times b \times h)$
or $\frac{1}{3}h(c^2 + cb + b^2)$.

Imagine the *yáng mǎ* cut exactly in half – the pieces are called *bié 'nào* or *turtle's shoulder joint*.

- What properties of the *yáng mǎ* and *bié 'nào* can you discover?
- Make some of the pieces, build them into blocks, give them names and find their volumes.

  Example: Take the cube as 1 unit; the wedge is $\frac{1}{2}$ unit;
  the *yáng mǎ* is $\frac{1}{3}$ unit.

A **roof** made of 2 wedges and 4 *yáng mǎ* is $2\frac{1}{3}$ units.
The **tunnel entrance** needs 2 turtle shoulder joints and a wedge.

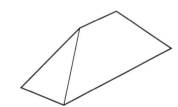

A roof or fodder loft

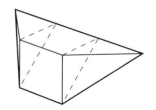

A tunnel or tomb entrance

7.5

Cylinders and circles

Ancient Egypt: Find the volume of a cylindrical granary of diameter 9 and height 10.
Take away $\frac{1}{9}$ of 9, namely 1; the remainder is 8.
Multiply 8 times 8; it makes 64.
Multiply 64 times 10; it makes 640 cubed cubits.

Ancient China: A circular hill fort.
Find the perimeter, square it.
Multiply by the height.
Find $\frac{1}{12}$; that is the volume.

Twentieth century: Volume of a cylinder = $\pi r^2 h$; use a calculator.

Granary,
Fortress,
or Can?

1 Make the measurements you need on a cylinder. Work out the volume by each method. Comment on differences.

We do not know how the ancient methods were discovered, but a diagram in the Rhind Mathematical Papyrus suggests that an octagon was used to approximate a circle.

The scribe drew :

2 Draw this octagon in a 9 × 9 square and work out its area.

3 Draw a circle which exactly fits inside the same square. Compare it with the octagon by eye. Do they seem to be equal or is one slightly larger than the other?

In China, area was related to the circumference, but there is no hint of how this was worked out. We know that Archimedes, in Greece, proved the connection round about 300 BC. The diagrams below show two practical ways of doing it:

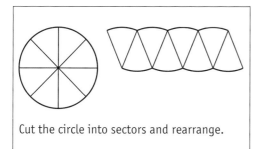

Cut the circle into sectors and rearrange.

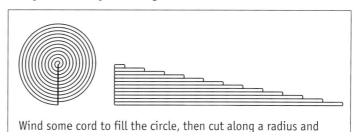

Wind some cord to fill the circle, then cut along a radius and straighten out the pieces.

4 Show that the 'rectangle' measures approximately $\frac{1}{2}$ circumference by $\frac{1}{2}$ diameter. In a similar way, find the base and height of the triangle of cord. How does this help to find the area of the circle?

5 Find a method for calculating the area of a sector of a circle if you know the diameter of the circle and the arc length of the sector.

Fingers for number symbols

For many centuries in Europe it was normal to show numbers on your hands rather than to write them down. The habit makes sense when writing materials are scarce. Very few people learned how to write anyway!

We have all used fingers for counting up to ten, but what then? In the Roman Empire people pointed to different joints of the finger and thumb for ten, twenty, thirty and so on. The left hand was used up to ninety and the right for hundreds.

This went on through medieval times. It must have been useful for international trade, when merchants and buyers might not understand each other's language. One of the first arithmetic books ever written in the English language shows these symbols in pictures.

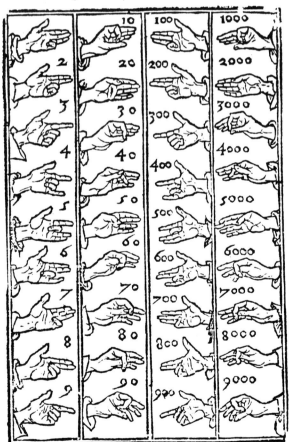

• Try to tell someone your age and then your phone number using these finger symbols.

Two great scholars of Anglo-Saxon Britain wrote about mathematics. Bede spent all his life in the monasteries at Monkwearmouth and Jarrow. His work on the calendar and on finger numbers is reckoned the best of his time.

Alcuin, a very different character, was born in the year that Bede died, AD 735. He was educated in York, but spent most of his life across the sea in Charlemagne's empire. Charlemagne called him over to help with a plan to offer some education to ordinary people.

One of Alcuin's efforts was a collection of mathematical puzzles. The original is lost, but this riddle may well be one of his:

I saw a man holding 8 in his hand, he took away 7, and 6 was left.

• Can you solve the riddle?

• Make up some more puzzles based on finger numbers.

Part 2 Europe wakes up to mathematics

Frontispiece from a translation and modification of Sacro Bosco's *Spherae Mundi* by Mauro of Florence (1537).

Introduction

Cardan, a man of the Renaissance

The Roman Empire and the Middle Ages which followed in Europe are notable for the lack of original work in mathematics. By contrast, developments continued in Islamic and Far Eastern regions. Then, in the so-called Renaissance, Europe woke up to mathematics in two respects. Scholars began to take an interest in solving new problems, and education, including some basic mathematics, became important to a much wider segment of the population.

The latter, involving practical applications of old mathematics, is particularly suitable for pupils of 10 to 16+. Social, economic, even political, connotations may be explored. There is plenty of material which is not too hard, but authors do tend to be wordy. Reluctantly, but realistically I feel for the purpose, I have drastically condensed much of their writing.

Three examples of 'new' mathematics from the same period are included. These are most suitable for post-16 students and comprise the advent of complex numbers, a theory of probability and universal gravitation.

Attitudes were profoundly affected by world exploration and progress in learning and technology. By AD 1700, astounding achievements of science, such as Newton's theory of gravity, had captured public imagination. We find, for instance, that mathematical puzzles, meant for general recreation, began to be published on a regular basis. In this era, known as the Enlightenment, traditional habits were questioned and in particular it began to be feasible for a woman to foster her mathematical talent.

In the classroom

Girolamo Cardano (1501–1576), a man of the Italian Renaissance, helps to set the scene very nicely at any level. Extracts from his autobiography are given on the sheet.

Ask pupils to find four things that excited Cardan (as he is often called) about the times in which he lived:

1 **Exploration of the world.** Vasco da Gama and Columbus had opened up new lands and seas; Magellan's voyages coincided with Cardan's youth.

2 **Gunpowder** had been known in China for many centuries, and used for both ceremonial and military purposes. Cannon were relatively new in the West. Cardan's century saw the development of a science of artillery plus the production of small arms.

3 **The magnetic compass** was hardly a new discovery, but was emerging as a significant aid to voyagers. Cardan himself had little experience of wild seas, though he once travelled as far as Scotland to treat the Bishop of St Andrews and achieved a successful cure. He records that the Bishop's request was backed up with the offer of '500 gold crowns of France on departure and 1200 upon return'.

4 **The printing press** encouraged an explosion of knowledge. Before long, not only were new developments published, but elementary books were written for a much wider audience. People such as navigators, traders, gunners, carpenters, surveyors, instrument-makers, government officials and so on needed more education to cope with the expanding world. In mathematics there was a demand for textbooks, written in the vernacular, which would explain elementary geometry and arithmetic and their applications.

Ask pupils to reflect on our own century, perhaps for homework followed by class discussion:

What will you tell your grandchildren about what was new and exciting in your times?

Which of these modern novelties relate in some way to mathematics?

Cardan led a troubled life, knowing both wealth and poverty, fame and hostility. What can pupils tell from the rest of the sheet about the scope of his work? The range of his knowledge is typical of a Renaissance scholar. He studied law and medicine, took a Doctorate in Medicine at the third attempt, but was initially excluded from the College of Physicians in Milan.

Despite the setbacks, he achieved a high reputation as a doctor and lectured successfully in science and mathematics. His treatise on the fast-developing subject of algebra, the *Ars Magna*, was a masterpiece of its time. His life ended under another cloud, brought about by difficulties with his sons and an accusation of heresy against himself. He wrote his strange autobiography in his old age.

Cardan, a man of the Renaissance

I was born in this century in which the whole world became known. These discoveries are sure to lead to dreadful upheavals ... but meantime we shall rejoice.

For what is more amazing than fireworks? Or firearms that man has invented, so much more destructive than the lightning of the gods?

Nor of thee, O Great Compass, will I be silent! You guide us over huge oceans, through gloomy nights, and through the wild storms seafarers dread.

The fourth marvel is the invention of printing ...

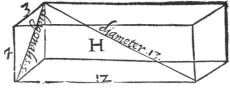

From *Practica Arithmetica*

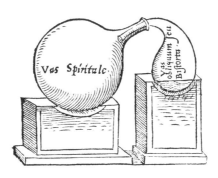

An idea for raising sunken ships. When stones are jettisoned from the small boats, the wreck lifts and can gradually be moved to shallower waters. From *De Subtilitate*.

Flasks for distillation

An idea for a lock. When the lettered disk spells SERPENS, cog wheels allow the lock to open, otherwise not. From *De Subtilitate*.

The Book of My Life

Chapter Five Stature and Appearance
I am a man of medium height; my feet are short, wide near the toes, and rather too high at the heels, so that I can scarcely find shoes to fit ...

Chapter Eighteen Things in Which I Take Pleasure
Pens for writing please me greatly and I have spent more than twenty gold crowns on them ...

I enjoy swimming a little and fishing very much ...

Chapter Nineteen Gambling and Dicing
I gambled for many years – every day – I say it with shame. It was insults, injustice, poverty, betrayal, and backbiting that drove me to it ...

Chapter Forty Success in my Practice
Altogether I restored to health more than one hundred men given up as hopeless, at Milan, Bologna, and Rome.

Girolamo Cardano (1501–1576)

Time chart

Some events in Britain and the world

Cities of north Italy flourish in commerce and culture
Portugal and Spain exploring the world
States such as Yoruba and Zimbabwe flourish in Africa
1517 Martin Luther kindles the Protestant Reformation
Last flourishing of Aztec and Inca Empires
Chinese Ming Dynasty with mandarin bureaucracy
Suleyman the Magnificent rules the Ottoman Empire
1534 Henry VIII breaks with the Church of Rome
Continuing expansion of Muscovy (centred on Moscow)
In Paris, Peter Ramus promotes humanist thinking
1542 Mary becomes Queen of Scots
1547 Edward VI, third Tudor king of England
1553 Expedition to explore the NE passage. Accession of Mary I
1555 Muscovy Company founded for trade with Russia
1558 Elizabeth I becomes queen of England
1561 Reform of English coinage
1563 More Acts passed against enclosure of arable land
Moghul Empire in India. Africa suffers the slave trade
1576–78 Martin Frobisher seeks a north-west passage
1577–80 Francis Drake circumnavigates the globe
Persian Safavid Dynasty flourishes
1588 Defeat of the Spanish Armada
William Shakespeare writing

1603 James VI of Scotland becomes James I of England
1611 King James issues proclamation on value of coins
1618 Thirty Years War in Europe begins
1620 Pilgrim Fathers land in New England
1625 Charles I becomes king of Great Britain
1626 Dutch found New Amsterdam (New York)
1635 Royal Observatory founded at Greenwich
1642 Civil war in Britain, conflict in Ireland
1649 Charles I beheaded, Cromwell leads

1654 Louis XIV crowned, royal domination in France
1660 Restoration of British monarchy, Charles II
1662 Royal Society founded
1665–66 Plague rampant, Cambridge University closed
1666 Great Fire of London
Manchu Empire dominates China and beyond

1685 Edict of Nantes revoked. Accession of James II
1689 Protestants take British throne: William and Mary

1700 Isaac Newton becomes Master of the Mint
1702 Queen Anne, last of the Stuarts
1714 George I, first Hanoverian monarch
1727 Newton dies in March; George II accedes in June
1745 Jacobite uprising, General Roy plans to map Scotland
1756 Seven Years War begins
1760 George III
1776 American Declaration of Independence
1789 French Revolution. Washington president of USA
1791 Ordnance Survey founded

1500
1550
1600
1650
1700
1750
1800

Some mathematical events related to the text

1501 Birth of Girolamo Cardano

1541 Tartaglia applies maths to artillery science
1543 Recorde's English arithmetic, *The Ground of Arts*
1545 Cardan's algebra masterpiece, *Ars Magna*
1546 Tartaglia seeks Henry VIII's patronage

1557 Robert Recorde, *The Whetstone of Witte*

1570 Billingsley's English 'Euclid', preface by Dee
1572 Rafael Bombelli's *Algebra* published
1575 John Dee edits *The Ground of Arts*

1585 Stevin, in Holland, originates decimal fractions

1614 John Napier publishes first logarithm tables
1614 Norton edits Recorde and includes decimal fractions

1631 Norwood, *Trigonometrie, the Doctrine of Triangles*
1633 Time changes in magnetic variation recognised
1635 Babington, gunner and mathematics student, *Geometrie*
1637 Richard Norwood, *The Seaman's Practice*

1650 Leybourn's first book on surveying
1654 Pascal and Fermat exchange letters about chance
1657 Huygens publishes a treatise on probability

1665–66 Newton's prime years for invention

1687 *Philosophiae Naturalis Principia Mathematica*
1690 Leybourn, *Cursus Mathematicus*, containing 9 books

1704 The *Ladies' Diary* (an almanack) begins publication
1718 Abraham de Moivre, *The Doctrine of Chances*
1729 Motte's English translation of Newton's *Principia*
1738 De Moivre's 2nd edition includes theory of annuities
1748 Maria Gaetana Agnesi, *Instituzioni Analitiche*
1759 Émilie du Châtelet, Newton's *Principia* in French
1784 Great theodolite commissioned from Jesse Ramsden
1787 Surveyors establish cross-channel connection
1791 Mudge begins the British triangulation survey

Quadrants and artillery

Briefing

Angle is introduced as a measure of tilt, and as a measure of the angle between two directions, suitable for beginners. Ratios in similar triangles are then used for measuring heights and depths. This can involve scale drawing or with older pupils it serves as an introduction to trigonometric ratios.

Background

Nicolo TARTAGLIA was born around 1500 in northern Italy and died in Venice in 1557. He was an able mathematician and, coming from a poor family, was largely self-taught. He seems always to have earned a meagre living, mostly by teaching. Tartaglia enjoyed some fame after winning a mathematical contest. He had worked out how to solve certain types of cubic equation. Cardan wanted to know the method and invited Tartaglia to visit him, promising letters of introduction to a patron. Tartaglia was very reluctant to share his discovery, but eventually passed it on in a coded poem after swearing Cardan to secrecy. The promise seems to have been kept for many years, but was broken when Cardan included the method along with many developments of his own in the *Ars Magna*. The bitter row which followed was never resolved between the two men.

It is said that, as a boy, Nicolo suffered a sabre wound to the face during a battle for his home town of Brescia. The experience left him with a stammer and, surprisingly, he adopted the nickname Tartaglia, meaning 'The Stammerer', instead of his family name Fontana. It is a sign of the times that in youth he encountered sword fighting and in adulthood applied mathematics to the study of practical artillery, being one of the first to do so. The extracts on sheet 8.1 are taken from his book on the subject, which was in fact translated into English. Tartaglia also sent a copy to Henry VIII, again in a vain hope of sponsorship.[1]

In the classroom

Sheet 8.1 Angle as a measure of slope
Military applications of mathematics are as real now as then, so I make no apology for including this theme.
Some questions to ask:

Why place the instrument in the mouth of the cannons?

What is the difference between the two cannon pictures?

How many divisions are on the arc of the quadrant?

How accurately could they possibly measure the angle of tilt?

A practical activity: design and make your own 'slope-measurer'. A very quick way of doing this is to stick a thread onto a protractor, taking care that the sticky-tape is along the zero line and the thread is hanging from the centre. A blob of Blu-Tack or similar on the other end of the thread makes it into a plumb-line.

An illustration from 1674.

With this basic clinometer, pupils can measure some angles of slope, for instance the slope of the stairs by contact with the bannister rail. It can also be used for finding angles of elevation and depression.

Measurements are best made with one person holding the clinometer steady in position and another taking the reading. Then it is necessary to think about the interpretation of the reading. The thread hangs at the 90° mark when the edge is horizontal. Talk about 'turning through an angle from this horizontal'. So if the scale reads 70° you have turned through 20°.

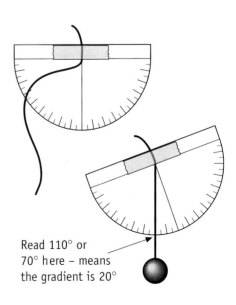

Read 110° or 70° here – means the gradient is 20°

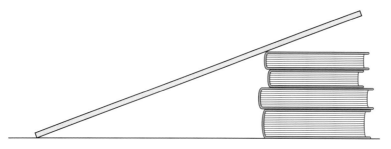

As an activity to gain further experience, pupils can set up a ruler or plank, propped on blocks or a chair, at what they judge to be a slope of 45° (or 10°, 25°, etc.). They then measure to test – they may be surprised.

Some more questions:

The picture at the bottom of sheet 8.1 is warning the gunner of a problem. What is it?

What could the fellow squinting at the castle be trying to do?

This question leads directly on to the next sheet.

Sheet 8.2 Measuring heights

A gunner rather than a mathematician wrote this English book in 1635. He shows an instrument which combines a square with a quadrant. Use the square if you want ratios, the quadrant if you want angles. Encourage pupils to read the seventeenth century script. They usually have fun with the ∫ for s. The exercises give practice in connecting the two scales: length on the square and angle on the quadrant.

Work on ratios. Pupils need to make their own cardboard square and to go and squint at some high object. Do a scale drawing or calculate:

As 18 is to 24
so *h* is to 12

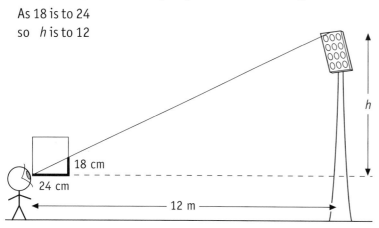

Add the eye height of the observer to *h* to find the height of the floodlights.

It is a good idea for several groups to measure the same object to get an idea of the range of experimental errors.

Work on trigonometry. This is a possibility with some classes. The ratio work gives a good grounding. Let pupils measure angles of elevation with the slope-measurer again. Learn to calculate results with 'tan'.

Sheet 8.3 Now depths and shadows

This is for consolidation. There is space to write in your own questions/instructions: maybe do some theoretical calculations, another practical when the sun shines, decipher the text, observe that drums were more common than paper in the army!

Sheet 8.4 Inaccessible distances

Discuss the first picture. The man in the foreground is using a Jacob's staff; the figures in the middle distance are using only their hats! In fact the two figures represent the same man. First he tilts his head until the brim of his hat appears to coincide with the opposite bank. Without altering this head-angle, he swings round until the brim coincides with some accessible ground. He paces out the distance to that point – which must be equal to the width of the river. The process depends on congruent triangles and can be carried out equally well with the staff. Pupils can try out the method and see what accuracy they achieve.

The questions get progressively harder, so choose whatever is suitable. The Chinese crag comes from an eighteenth-century encyclopaedia, but such problems appear in the *Sea Island Mathematical Manual* of Liu Hui.

Mathematics and artillery

Nicolo Tartaglia (*c.* 1500–1557)

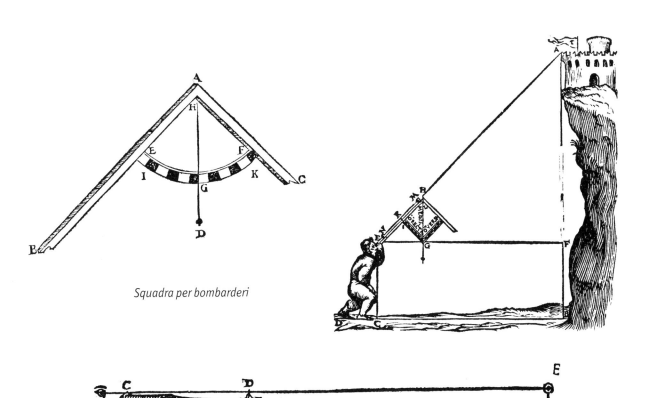

Squadra per bombarderi

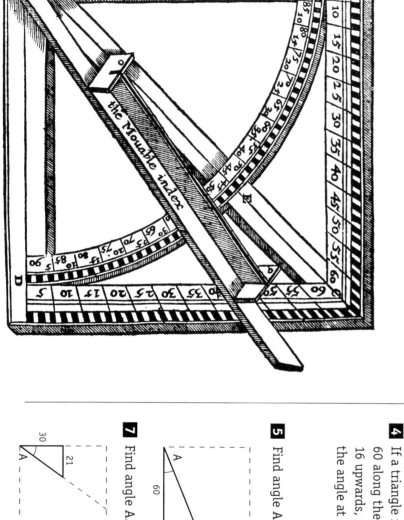

Gentle Reader,

His short Treatise of Geometry is not intended for such as are Masters of that Art, but onely for young practitioners, and more especially for my fellow Gunners, to whom it most properly belongeth,

Thy friend,

JOHN BABINGTON, Student in the Mathematikes.

The forme of the Geometricall Square.

BC and CD being divided each into sixtie equall parts. A being the centre, on which the moveable index playeth. BD a Quadrant divided into ninetie degrees and minutes, which is placed within the Square.

Intelligent Student,

What is John Babington telling you about this measuring instrument? How is it different from Tartaglia's?

Use your ruler as a movable index to find out:

1 The angle when the index lies on the diagonal.

2 The angle when the index goes to 35 on the top scale.

3 The angle when the index goes to 50 on the top scale.

4 If a triangle measures 60 along the base and 16 upwards, what is the angle at A?

5 Find angle A.

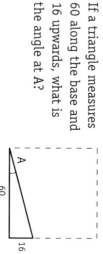

6 Find angle A.

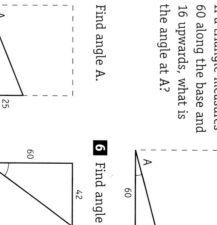

7 Find angle A.

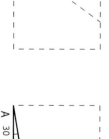

8 Find angle A.

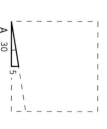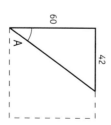

Depths by square and drum, heights by shadow

How to meafure all forts of profundities by the faid fquare.

IN meafuring all forts of profundities, the fquare muft be placed contrary to the aforefaid order ufed in taking of altitudes, that is the fide devided in the fquare, muft be turned downwards, whereas before it was upermoft, to take the profundity or depth of a Well, place your fquare on the top, fo that it may ftand horizontall, and likewife that fide next your eye may bee equall with the fide of the Orifice of the Well, then move the index, till through the fights you fee the bottome of the Well on the oppofite fide to your fquare, that done, obferve the parts cut in the fquare, which will be of right fhadow, and the rule will ftand thus: as the parts cut are to the whole fide, fo is the diameter of the Orifice to the depth of the Well.

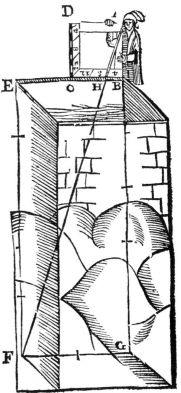

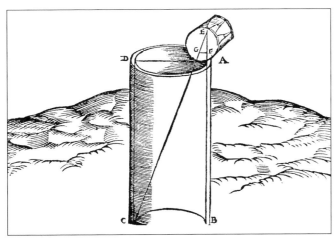

Della Profondita

Dell'altezza

Measuring the inaccessible

1 Describe how to find the width of the river without getting wet.

2 *To find the distance of any place inaccessible, by the Quadrant.*

Suppofe a Caftle placed at A, whofe diftance I defire to know in regard of placing my Ordnance, to make a batterie againft it.

First I make choice of a convenient place for my ftation, which is B, where placing my inftrument I bring the index to the edge or no degree, and fet it to point A. My inftrument ftanding quiet, I obferve the line BC in which I meafure out a hundred yards or at pleafure, then bring my inftrument to the point C, in fuch a manner that the edge may be parallel to the line BC.

Turning about the index until I fee the point A thorow the fight, I obferve the degrees cut in the Quadrant, and finde them to be feventy degrees, no minute, which I note.

How far away is the castle?

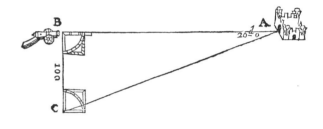

3 Chinese crag:
What measurements do you think were taken, and how could they be used to find the height of the crag?

4 Can you invent any other ways of measuring the inaccessible?

Arithmetike

Briefing

Robert Recorde was the most noted expositor of arithmetic in England during the sixteenth century. Extracts from his works can be used in several ways:

1 As part of a project on Tudor England, particularly to give an angle on education, and touching such issues as sheep and coinage.

2 To contrast arithmetic then and now. Then it was often a subject studied first by adults; counting boards vied with pencil and paper; Hindu–Arabic notation was a novelty; and decimal fractions gained only slow acceptance. Weights and measures were a morass.

3 To pick up and work on snippets of mathematics:
summing progressions
conversion between units, especially money
percentage change
multiplication (a method for 6× to 9× tables)
squares, cubes and powers
computation with decimals.

Background

obert RECORDE, or Record (both spellings are used), was born in Tenby, south Wales, about 1510. He was amongst the first to write mathematics textbooks in the English language, at a time when the propriety of producing books in the vernacular was a live issue. His arithmetic book, *The Ground of Arts* (1543), became phenomenally successful, running to at least 45 editions during a period of 150 years.

In Recorde's day, the ability to read, write and converse in Latin was the mark of an educated person. Grammar schools were preoccupied with teaching Latin grammar. Basic literacy in English could be acquired in 'petty schools' and scriveners offered tuition in the keeping of accounts, but mathematics as such had no assured place in the curriculum of schools nor of the bachelor degree. The medieval traditions of the universities were being influenced by the new humanist thinking, but mathematics was not highly regarded and when Henry VIII came to establish new chairs at Cambridge and Oxford, the subjects he chose were civil law, Greek,

Hebrew, physick (medicine) and theology. Only a few individuals studied and taught mathematics, generally for their own interest.

Study at the university, still central for scholars and churchmen, was also becoming a route to social advancement, executive positions and tutoring the children of nobility. Such was the career of Recorde.

He first graduated at the age of about nineteen, which was normal at that time. After a few years he took a doctorate in medicine, then practised as a physician in London. In 1549 he was appointed comptroller of the Bristol Mint. These were tricky times and Recorde made an enemy of Sir William Herbert, which led to a brief imprisonment. Later he obtained an appointment as General Surveyor of Mines and Monies in Ireland. This too was disastrous, since the mines failed to make any profit. According to one report Recorde sold meat intended for the miners, profiteered in the sale of herrings and grain, established a monopoly in shoes which were sold at inflated prices, borrowed money, failed to pay bills and so on.[1] According to another report, when Recorde returned to London he was owed more than £1000 by the government![2] He clashed again with Herbert, now the powerful Earl of Pembroke, and appears to have ended his days in prison in 1558.

By then he had published four (possibly five) of the intended six volumes in his series of mathematics texts. The choice of material and the care with which it is expounded suggest that Recorde had some experience as a tutor. *The Ground of Arts* introduces Hindu–Arabic notation, the four rules for whole numbers, various applications including money, weights and measures, ratio and proportion. In later editions, fractions are also taught and applied to the same range of topics. The second part of the book is devoted to arithmetic with the counting board, a device that was very commonly used in commerce. *The Pathway to Knowledge* is a geometry book, taking a much more pragmatic approach than Euclid. Then came two books dedicated to the governors etc. of the 'companie of venturers into Moscovia', i.e. the Muscovy Company: *The Castle of Knowledge*, which concerns basic astronomy, and, finally, *The Whetstone of Witte*, which contains more advanced arithmetic and some algebra, known as the 'art of cossike number'.

After Recorde's demise, *The Ground of Arts* had many editors including John DEE (1527–1608), a talented scholar. John was the son of a London mercer, one of the new 'middle class', involved in the profitable textile trade. John Dee was widely travelled and influential in many fields: certainly he stimulated interest in the mathematical arts in England. His preface to the first English translation of Euclid (by Henry Billingsley) set out the value and applications of mathematics. This preface was widely read and discussed. John Aubrey (1627–1691), the racy biographer, recounts:

> *Hee had a very faire cleare rosie complexion; a long beard as white as milk; he was tall and slender; a very handsome man … Old Goodwife Faldo did know Dr Dee … She sayd he kept a great many Stilles goeing. That he layd the storme. That the children dreaded him because he was accounted a Conjuror.*

The reputation of being a magician was a serious matter and Dee ended his life somewhat discredited on that account. Subsequent editors of Recorde's book were perhaps not so distinguished, but they made additions, and kept it up to date, so that it remained popular with all who wanted a useful grounding in arithmetic.

In the classroom

Sheet 9.1 Introduction and discussion

For pupils aged 13 and upwards, there are six short extracts from *The Ground of Arts*. Pupils can work on them in small groups, reporting back to the whole class on the piece they have interpreted.

The following points might emerge in discussion:

1 The spelling is weird, but intelligible if you go by the sound of words. The genuine font, reproduced for the table of English coins, is hard on the modern eye.

2 The book is written as a conversation between Master and Scholar, and is much more wordy than most arithmetic books today. Perhaps this was helpful for an adult studying alone without a tutor?

3 Hindu–Arabic numerals seem to have been a novelty which had to be explained in terms of Roman numerals. The place value concept and the cypher required explanation.

4 Recorde used topical examples, in this case about sheep raised for the profitable wool trade. Despite the supposed law, enclosure of land for grazing caused hardship in the countryside. Can pupils find any political/social assumptions in their own maths textbooks?

5 Coins and measures are unfamiliar; more about this on sheets 9.2 and 9.5.

6 A rule for summing arithmetic progressions is given without reasons, but it is apparent to common sense. Can pupils explain it in simple words? The rule is to find the average size of a term and multiply by the number of terms. Recorde's general tutoring principle was to consolidate the rule first and reserve the explanation.

7 There do not seem to be any exercises. True, but practice was expected: 'Yea but you must prove yourself to do some things that you were never taught, or else you shall not be able to do any more than you were taught, and were rather to learn by rote than by reason.'

8 Counting boards were common for calculation. In this type, the counters on successive horizontal lines stood for thousands, hundreds, tens and units. Counters between the lines stood for 5 of each.

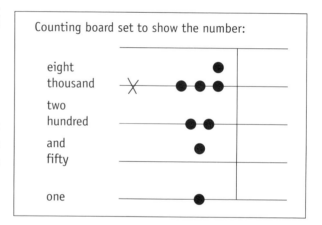

Counting board set to show the number:
eight thousand
two hundred
and fifty
one

Various of the mathematical points may be developed, according to the demands of your syllabus.

Sheet 9.2 More about 'English coynes'

This is possible even for younger pupils: the data shows changes between the first edition in 1543 and the 1614 edition of *The Ground of Arts*.

List the gold coins of 1543. Then put them in order of monetary value. Do the same for silver and try some hypothetical buying and selling. For instance, to pay for a wool cap worth 1 shilling you could use 3 groats or 4 harps or 8 dandyprattes!

Debased coinage. Towards the end of his reign, when short of funds, Henry VIII made money by mixing alloy with his coins. There was a particularly severe reduction in the proportion of precious metal in his silver coins. Wars, trade and the supply of gold and silver continued to affect coinage everywhere. Some of the impact of this can be seen in the second half of the sheet, which is taken from Recorde's 1614 edition.

List some of the changes. Calculate the percentage increase in the accounted value of the old gold coins i.e. Great Sovereign, Royal, Old Noble, Angel and George Noble (approximately 50% in each case). The debased sovereigns of King Henry and Elizabeth were worth very much less in terms of shillings and pence. Coins themselves did not begin to have a value marked on them until the time of James I and VI. It was he who issued this 1611 proclamation.

Smaller amounts. Of course, the silver halfpenny was too valuable for many transactions and traders tended to issue tokens for local use. James also experimented with brass farthings to overcome this problem. Recorde gives these 'Figures of money':

c	a cee the xvi ($\frac{1}{16}$ penny)	d	a pennie
q	a kewe the viii ($\frac{1}{8}$ penny)	s	a shilling
$\tilde{q}$	a farthing the iiii ($\frac{1}{4}$ penny)		
ob	a halfe pennie	℔	a pound

Sheet 9.3 The 'harder' times tables

What do pupils make of the illustration? Counting boards were common. More go-ahead merchants would do reckoning with figures. No wonder that tables above the 5× were regarded as hard. Let pupils try Recorde's method on lots of examples.[3] Does it help?

A much harder task is to explain why the method works. This requires an understanding of place value and some algebra. For instance, if we take $(10-x)$ and $(10-y)$ to be the numbers, then x and y are the 'differences'. The method consists of putting the product xy in the units position and the difference $(10 - x) - y$ or $(10 - y) - x$ ('which you will for all is like'!) in the tens position. Then it is only a matter of manipulation to show

that $10(10 - x - y) + xy$ is actually the product of the two original numbers $(10-x)(10-y)$.

Sheet 9.4 Powers, squares, cubes and beyond

Pupils should read the dialogue, which is interesting both for the naming of the powers and for their representations. Zenzizenzike[4] sounds more fun than quartic! Ask pupils to invent their own names for higher powers and to represent them as they choose. Note that a cubic cube is the sixth power, whereas a zenzizenzizenzike number is presumably a squared square of squares which would be the eighth power. Recorde did not have index notation, but this would be a good time to introduce it.

Sheet 9.5 Early days of decimals

This is suitable for older pupils to discuss, perhaps to prompt computation practice. Recorde's 1614 editor, Robert Norton, was a professional gunner and engineer in the Tower of London. He had translated Stevin's *Disme* from the Dutch. Here he uses a similar notation to Stevin's and adopts his idea of primes (tenth parts), seconds (hundredth parts) and so on. It is interesting that the next editor, Robert Hartwell, dropped this section again. Questions for pupils might be:

What was different about Leybourn's[5] attitude and approach by 1690?

What progress have we made with units of measurement? Why has metrication been slow? (Scope for a project here: it was only in 1971 that UK coinage was decimalized!)

The Ground of Arts by Robert Recorde

 umeration is that Arithmeticall skill, whereby we may duely value, expresse and read any summe proposed or else in apte figures sette downe any Number. **Scholar**. Why? then me thinketh you put a difference betwene the value and the figure.

Master. Yea so doe I: for the value is one thing, and the figures are another thing, and that commeth chiefly of the places wherein they be set. And first marke, that there are but ten figures that are used in Arithmetik: and of those ten, one doth signify nothing, which is made like an o, and is called a Cypher. The other nyne are called signifying figures, and be thus figured,

1	2	3	4	5	6	7	8	9

and this is their value

i.	ii.	iii.	iiii.	v.	vi.	vii.	viii.	ix.

But here you must mark, that every figure hathe two values: One always certaine, that it signifyeth properly, which it hath of his forme. And the other uncertayne whiche he taketh of his place.

S. There is supposed a lawe made that (for furtheryng of tyllage) every man that doth kepe shepe, shall for every 10 shepe, eare and sowe one acre of grounde ... and the shepe are waxen so fierce nowe and so myghte, that none can withstande them but the lyon.

M. I perceave you talke as you hear some other, but to the work of your question.

... for the measures of ale are as foloweth

of ale $\left\{\begin{array}{l}\text{the fyrken}\\ \text{ye kilderkyn}\\ \text{the barrel}\end{array}\right\}$ containeth $\left\{\begin{array}{l}8\\16\\32\end{array}\right\}$ gallons

Sope measures, both fyrken, kylderkyn, and barrell, shulde be all equall to Ale measures. Morover the statutes dooth lymytte the weight of every of those thre vessels beyng empty.

$\left.\begin{array}{l}\text{A barrel}\\ \text{Halfe barell}\\ \text{A fyrken}\end{array}\right\}$ to wey empty $\left\{\begin{array}{l}26\\13\\6\frac{1}{2}\end{array}\right\}$ pound.

Hearrynges also be solde by the same measures ... Salmon and eeles have a greater measure.

Progression is a breefe and quicke addition of divers summes ...

S. I understande you not well.

M. By an exaumple I wyll be playner: 1, 2, 3, 4, 5, 6, here you see the seconde to dyffre from the fyrste but by 1, and so doeth all the other.

S. This I perceave.

M. And lykewayes here: 4, 7, 10, 13, 16, 19, 22, 25.

S. Yea, then procede by the difference of 3.

M. And so I meane, that Progressions is an art how to adde al such numbres muche quicklyer than by common Addytion. As in this example, 2, 4, 6, 8, 10, 12, 14, where the numbres are 7, therefore set downe 7 in a place alone: then adde togyther the fyrst numbre and the laste, as in this example: adde 2 to 14, and that maketh 16, take halfe of it and multiplye by ye 7, whiche you noted: 8 multiplied by 7 make 56, and yt is the summe of all ye figures.

S. That will I prove by another example: I would know how much this summe is 5, 8, 11, 14, 17, 20, 23, 26, 29.

A table for English coynes. Anno. 1540.	
A Soueraynne.	A quarter Noble.
Halfe a Soueraynne.	A Croune.
A Royall.	Halfe a Croune.
Halfe a Royall.	A croune.
A quarter Royall.	A Grote.
An olde Noble.	A harpe Grote.
Halfe an olde Noble.	A penny of 2 pens.
An Angell.	A dandy pratte.
Halfe an Angell.	A penny.
A George Noble.	An halfe pennie.
Halfe a George Noble.	A Farthing.

Nowe that you have learned the common kyndes of Arithmetike with the penne, you shall see the same arte in counters: whiche feate dooeth not onely serve for theym that can not write and read, but also for them that can do bothe, but have not at some tymes their penne or tables ready with them ... if you wolde add 2659 to 8342, you must sette your summes as you se here. And then if you lyst, you mai adde the one to the other in ye same place, or els you may adde them togyther in a newe place ...

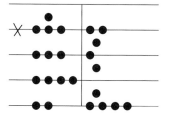

The value of English coins

1543

A Sovereign is the greatest English coin, and contains 2 Royals or
3 Angels, either 9 half crowns, or 4 crowns and an half, that is to say 22s 6d.

Gold crown minted
in Recorde's lifetime

- Half a Sovereign is equal with a Royal.
- A Royal contains an Angel and half, that is to say, 11s 3d.
- Half a Royal contains 5s 7d ob.
- A quarter of a Royal contains 2 shillings 9d ob q̄.
- An old Noble, called a Henry, is worth two crowns, or a noble and half, that is 10s.
- Half an old noble is worth 5s.
- An angel contains a crown and half, that is 7s 6d.
- Half an angel is worth 3s 9d.
- A Noble, called a George, is worth 6s 8d.
- Half a Noble is worth 3s 4d.
- A Crown contains 5s and the half crown 2s 6d.
- How be it there is another crown of 4s 6d. ...

An illegal Bristol token of 1567,
inscribed with the name of
John Brown, Grocer

Abbreviations
s = shilling
d = pence
ob = halfpenny
q̄ = farthing

In silver, the greatest is the Groat, which contains 4 pennies. Then is there another Groat called an Harp, which goes for 3d. Then next is the penny of 2d, and then a dandypratte worth three half pennies. Next is a penny, then a half penny, and last and least of all a farthing.

... but yet of the two most common values of money spake I nothing, that is to say, of pounds and shillings, which though they have no coins, yet is there no name more in use than they, of which the shilling contains 12 pennies or 3 groats, and the pound, 2 old Nobles, 3 George Nobles, or 4 crowns, that is to say 20s. And this is now the rate of English money.

1614

Some valuations by the Kings Majesties Proclamation for Gold, Dated the 23. of November, 1611.

	Shil.	Pence.
Great Sovereign	33	0
Royal	16	6
Old Noble	14	8
Angel	11	0
George Noble	9	9 ob.
Sover. King Henry best	11	8 ob.q̄
Sovereign King Henry	11	0
Elizabeth Sover.	11	0
Elizabeth Crown	5	6

Of Silver Coins current in this Realm.

- The Edward Crown of 5s.
- The Edward half Crown of 2s 6d.
- The Edward Shilling, half Shilling, and the threepence.
- Philip and Mary's Shilling, and half Shilling.
- The Mary Groat, and Mary two pence.
- Queen Elizabeth's Shilling, 6d, 4d, 3d, 2d, 1d, three farthings, and half penny.

1551 Edward VI silver
crown, first English coin
of 4 cm diameter, issued
as pledge of reform after
Henry's debasement

Machine struck
shilling of Elizabeth I.
The screw press was
later banned because
coiners were being
forced out of work.

Complementary multiplication

MVLTIPLICATION
I thynke befte to fhewe you fyrfte the arte of multiplying digettes ... And as for the fmal digettes under 5, it were but folly to teach any rule, feyng thei are fo easy, yt every child can doo it.

Abacist and algorist

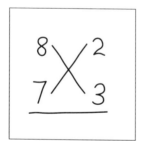

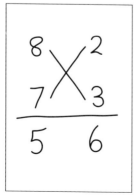

But for the multiplication of the greater digits, thus shall you do. First set your digits one over the other digit, then from the uppermost downward, and from the nethermost upward, draw straight lines, so that they make a cross commonly called saint Andrews cross, as you see here: as if I would know how many are 7 times 8, I must write those digits thus.

Then do I look how much 8 doth differ from 10, and I find it to be 2, that 2 do I write at the right hand of 8, at the end of the line, thus. After that I take the difference of 7 likewise from 10, that is 3, and I write that at the right side of 7, as you see in this example. Then do I draw a line under them, as in addition, thus.

Last of all I multiply the two differences as saying: 2 times 3 makes 6, that must I enter under the differences, beneath the line: then must I take the one of the differences (which I will, for all is like) from the other digit (not from his own) as the lines of the cross warn me, and that which is left must I write under the digits. As in this example. If I take 2 from 7, or 3 from 8, there remaineth 5: ye 5 must I write under ye digits: and then there appeared the multiplication of 7 times 8 to be 56. And so likewise of any other digits if they be above 5.

9.4

Square, cube and zenzizenzike numbers

Master. 3 times 3 maketh 9 which is a *square number*, and is represented thus. ●●● ●●● ●●●

Next are *Cubike numbers*; which are produced by triple multiplication. As 2 times 2 twice, maketh 8. And 3 times 3 thrice yields 27. So 4 times 4 four times giveth 64. These numbers can not be expressed aptly in flatte, but prospectively, as Dice.

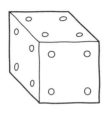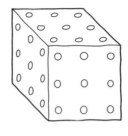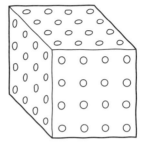

In the first figure you see '2 expressed in lengthe, breadthe and depthe' and so on.

But to proceed, if you do multiply that *Cubike number* by his root, the number that riseth of it, is called a *square of squares* commonly, which numbers I do call *long Cubes*: because they make a line of Cubes ... And of some men they are named *Zenzizenzikes*, as square numbers are called *Zenzikes*.

Scholar. So I understand that 16 is a number of that sort. Likewise 64 is a square number, and hath for his root 8. Again 64 is a *Cubike number*, and hath for his root 4.

Master. You say truth. Although the last example be not to your purpose, concerning *Zenzizenzikes*.

Scholar. So I see, wherefore I might rather have taken 81 which is a *Zenzizenzike number*, and so hath for his root 3. And also a square number, and hath 9 for his root.

Master. Farther to proceed, if I multiply those *Zenzizenzike numbers* by their root, they will make *Sursolide numbers* ... And so you may increase the numbers according to the times of your multiplication as much as you list.

And every order shall bear such names, as agreeth to the nature of their roots.

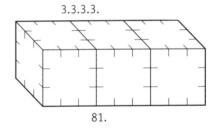

Eighty-one as a long cube

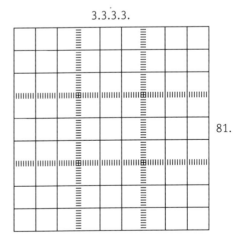

Eighty-one as a square of squares, or zenzizenike number

Decimal Arithmetick

The Ground of Arts, Robert Recorde, 1543

Wherefore to the intent that you may have a light knowledge in the common weights and measures ... Now will I show you, after the Statutes of England, where the least portion of weight is commonly a grain, meaning a grain of corn or wheat, dry, and gathered out of the middle of the ear.

Now again there are greater weights which are called a hundred, half a hundred, and a quarterne ... a hundred is not just 100, but 112 pound ... How be it there are in some things other names: as in wool, 28 pounds is not called a quaterne but a todde, and the 14 pound is not named a half quaterne but a stone.

But now remaineth yet another kind of measure, whereby men mete length and breadth. 3 grains of barley make an inch. 12 inches make a foot. 3 foot make a yard. 5 yards and half make a perch.

Cursus Mathematicus, William Leybourn, 1690

Who was the first to invent this Decimal Arithmetick ... is hard to determine, but that it hath been much improved since the Invention of Logarithms, all knowing Artists cannot but Acknowledge, and that at this day it is arrived to the Zenith of its perfection.

And indeed this excellent kind of Arithmetick might be yet farther improved, if all our Coins, Weights, and Measures were divided and sub-divided Decimally.

The Integers and Decimal Fractions are distinguished each from other several ways, according to several Mens fancies; but the general received way, if you were to set down $763 \frac{7627}{10000}$ is 763.7626

Some would express it thus 763|7626 or thus 763.7′6″2‴6⁗ or thus 763|7626 etc.

The Ground of Arts, 1625 edition

The new additions here followeth by Mr. R. N. both plaine, pithy and profitable:

Sir I have heard of a new application of Arithmetick, which is called decimal Arithmetick, I desire you to shew me what it is and the use and operation thereof; because I have heard it much commended for avoiding of all fractions.

Master ... As in measure of land, the principal measure being the perch, shall first be divided into ten equal parts or primes, and again each prime shall be divided into ten equall parts or seconds.

Scholar. I pray you sir shew the difference betweene the addition of such tenthes, and the vulgar addition of whole numbers.

Master. There can be no difference shewed therein. For suppose you are to Adde 31 perches $5^1\,7^2\,2^3$ unto 91 perches $4^1\,3^2\,8^3$ you shall find by setting them in this manner and having added them according to the ordinary fashion that the total sum will amount.

$$315^1\,7^2\,2^3$$
$$91438$$
$$\overline{123010}$$

Scholar. But how is multiplication performed: I suppose that, and division should be more difficult, for the former are exceeding plain?

Master. There is no more hardness in them than in the former, for you shall set down all the parts as if they were whole numbers and work them accordingly, only this you must observe that having finished your multiplication, you shall add the last sign of the multiplier to the last sign of the multiplicant and the total thereof shall be the last sign of the product.

Navigating the oceans

Briefing

When pupils study the great voyages of discovery, why not add a mathematical component? A simple introduction involves compass points and speed by the log-line. For more advanced pupils, use vector ideas to allow for currents.

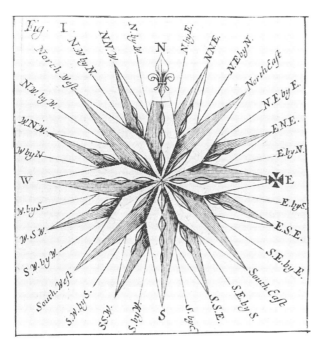

Background

An experienced seaman could sail in coastal waters or make familiar sea crossings with only the most basic navigational aids, but exploration of unknown routes and long ocean voyages were a different matter. After weeks and months at sea, how was the ship's captain to know his position and set his course?

When John Cabot returned to Bristol after his historic landing in the New Found Land in 1497, there was a flurry of Atlantic journeys. But no route to fabled Cathay was found, and for the remaining first half of the sixteenth century, English sailors were scarcely involved in world exploration. Few made the effort to learn skills of charting, observing stars, moon and sun, or to master mathematical calculation.

Meanwhile Spain and Portugal forged ahead. However, by 1553, with Edward VI on the throne, London sponsors were found for an expedition to investigate the north-east. Willoughby, with two of the three ships, went off course and was lost in the icy seas, but Chancellor,

who had been tutored by John Dee,[1] managed to open up a route through the White Sea to Moscow. Soon after his return, the Muscovy Company was set up with exclusive rights to Russian trade.

Gradually attitudes changed and expertise was developed. Skilled engravers began to make an impressive range of instruments. Scales were divided with sufficient accuracy for angles to be read to minutes rather than whole degrees. A wide spectrum of people, from university men to retired seamen, set up as practical mathematics teachers, and very often designed their own instruments. As the navy and the merchant fleets grew during Elizabeth's reign, there was a good demand for their services.

Richard NORWOOD (1590–1675)[2] was one who went to sea as a young man, then turned teacher and author. He settled for a while on Tower Hill, an area of London close to the Navy Office which was popular amongst mathematical practitioners. During this period he undertook a notable survey up to York in order to determine the size of the earth more accurately. In later life he lived in the Bermudas, where he continued teaching and occasionally surveying.

In the classroom

Sheet 10.1 provides an elementary starting point. **Sheet 10.2**, about vector addition of distances, is more advanced. In either case it would be appropriate to start by sketching the historical scene.

Sheet 10.1 Compass points, bearings, and estimating speeds

Pupils can draw their own set of compass points, choosing whether to go for the basic N, S, E and W only, or for 8, 16 or even 32 points. Connect the compass points with bearings, e.g. the direction NE is the same as the bearing 045° and NW is 315°.

Set up real compasses and note the direction of 'landmarks' in the classroom and the school.

What problems might the ship's navigator have with his compass? Pitching about on the waves could be overcome by the gimbal mounting, which allowed the needle to remain horizontal.[3] The other main problem was magnetic variation. If anyone wants to know about variation, a recent Ordnance Survey map should give the difference between true north and magnetic north for the area. It will also indicate how the variation is expected to change over the next few years.

What was a log-line? In fact it was simply a log on the end of a rope.[4] Pupils should read Norwood's explanation of the timing. The log was thrown overboard and, if the sailor managed to reel out the line fast enough, the log stayed roughly stationary in the water. The idea was to measure the length of line reeled out whilst counting 30 seconds. That length equalled the distance the ship had travelled forwards in 30 seconds, hence the speed. Pupils could try to explain the method in their own words to the new cabin boy. In practice, lines were knotted and if this was done at crafty intervals, all you needed to do was count the knots.

Why do pupils think the log-line was an uncertain method? In addition to the uncertainties, quoted on the sheet, the timing also tended to be imprecise. Even sophisticated mariners, using a sand glass, found that with frequent use the sand wore a larger hole and then ran through too fast! Pupils should read what Norwood says about it – on which points did they agree?

Pupils can follow through Norwood's calculation. This particular example gives a speed of one mile in an hour, but they should remember that this was a nautical mile, different from a statute mile. A nautical mile is supposed to be the length of an arc on the earth's surface which subtends an angle of 1 minute ($\frac{1}{60}$ of 1 degree) at the earth's centre. The actual length of a nautical mile was another uncertain matter! Norwood reckoned 6120 feet on the basis of his measurement of the distance from London to York. His was a remarkably accurate value (less than 1% error) in comparison with the 5000 feet commonly used at the time. If pupils were advising the Captain, would they say that the true speed was more or less than 1 nautical mile per hour? Remember that he will not be pleased to come unexpectedly upon land – better late than sorry, but not too late! Devise some more log-line calculations.

Do exercises on currents for practice on East and West and directed numbers. Draw diagrams and make up some more examples.

A project. Pupils could make their own measurements to determine the length of a nautical mile, or, in other words, the size of the earth. One way of doing this is to sight the pole star with a clinometer (chapter 8) from two different places, or negotiate with someone else to make one of the sightings. These places must be a measurable distance apart in a N–S direction. Since 70 miles will make a difference of only about 1°, the further apart

the better. The diagram illustrates the principle: the difference between the sightings at P and Q is equal to the angle A at the centre of the earth.

As Norwood states, navigation also requires knowledge of latitude and longitude. Two excellent sources for following this up are given in the notes.[5]

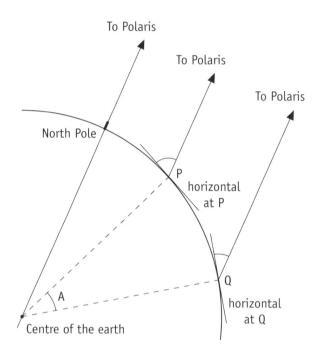

Sighting the pole star.

Sheet 10.2 Vector addition

To allow for current in general requires a simple idea of relative velocity. Add the velocity of the water to the velocity of the ship through the water to get the ship's true velocity. This sheet is basically an exercise in trigonometry in a nautical context. Knowledge of right-angled triangles is sufficient but question 8 is easier by sine formula.

The wording is Norwood's, occasionally abbreviated. There seems little point in trying to take pupils through his demonstrations which use logsin tables. Instead they have the task of modernizing the calculations!

Modern mariners and aircraft pilots are able to make very precise checks that their route is working out as planned. Radio signals from satellites give a 'navigational fix' and computers, programmed of course to take account of currents or wind, provide the optimum heading.

The Seaman's Practice by Richard Norwood 1637

There be four things upon which the Practice of Navigation is efpecially grounded, namely, the Knowledg of the Longitude, Latitude, Courfe and Diftance.

Course: The courfe is fet by the compafs, the variation being duly obferved.

Distance: The Diftance run, is found by the Log-line.

Now fuppofing the Time of the running out of the Log-Line to be meafured by a half-minute Glafs, if we obferve how many Feet or Fathoms fhe runs in half a Minute, we may thereby find her way* for an hour.

*'way' means rate of progress through the water.

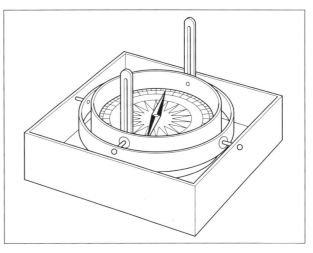

A ship's compass mounted on two brass rings (gimbals). An early example of this type was found on the *Mary Rose*, sunk outside Portsmouth in 1545.

As, admit there runs out of the Log-line in half a minute's space 51 Feet, or $8\frac{1}{2}$ Fathoms, and you would know what way the Ship makes every Hour after the same Rate: say by the Rule of Proportion.

> If $0\frac{1}{2}$ Minute gives 51 Feet, what give 60 Minutes? Or,
> If 1 Minute give 102 Feet, what give 60 Minutes?
> And so, multiplying, you shall find 6120 Feet, which is one Mile.

And although he which veers the Log-line be careful to overhale it so slack, that it may not draw forward the Log, yet (no doubt) it doth lose some way, following the Ship a little as it is drawn by the Line, and withal by the Eddy of the Ship's wake, and sometimes also is cast forwards by the Wind and Waves, when they come after the Ship ... such allowance may be made for it as a Man in his Experience and Discretion shall think fit.

...the Ship's way is commonly more than by the Log-line it appears to be, and every Man desires...that he fall not with a Place unexpected.

Ark Royal, flagship from the battle with the Spanish Armada

Currents:

1 Admit a Current run East 3 Miles an Hour, and that a Ship under Sail run West directly against it 6 Miles an Hour. What is her true or compound Motion?

2 Admit a Current run West 6 Miles an Hour, and that a Ship under Sail run directly against it 5 Miles an Hour by the Log: What is the Ship's compound Motion, and which way?

3 Admit a Current run East 3 Miles an Hour, and the Ship also run East 3 Miles an Hour by the Log; What is the Ship's true motion?

The Seaman's Practice (1637) – Currents

Chap. XII … yet feeing it is neceffary in *Navigation* to take notice of Currents, and to make competent Allowance for them; I will briefly fet down certain *Problems*, fuch as I have fometimes thought upon, whereby a Man may judge of that allowance, for I know not any that have handled it.

Firft then, it is to be conceived, that a Ship, or other Veffel failing or rowing where there is a Current, hath a compound motion arifing of two different Principles; namely, of the Current and the Ship's way. The compound of them, is the Line of the Ship's true Motion.

Richard Norwood demonstrated how to solve the following problems by trigonometry, which had been known for a long time. To save some labour in calculating, he used logarithm tables, recently invented by Lord Napier of Merchiston (near Edinburgh).

• Draw diagrams and show how you would solve some of these problems, adding more examples of your own.

4 Admit a Current run East 2 Miles an Hour, and the Ship South six Miles an Hour: What is the Ship's true motion and which way?

5 A Ship sails West 5 days together, by the Log 725 Miles: but there is a Current all this while setting to the Southwards $1\frac{1}{2}$ Miles an Hour: I demand how she hath sailed, and how far?

12 To find where there is a Current at Sea; also which way it sets, and how fast.

This may be done by comparing the Reckoning outwards with the Reckonings homewards, whereof we shall give an Example.
Admit a Ship sail from Bermudus till she arrive at Cape Cod in New England. Then by the Courses and distances we may gather by the following Table, that Cape Cod should by this Reckoning be to the Northwards 487 miles, and to the Westwards 30 miles.
Now suppose she sail back again and the Courses and distances appeareth, Bermudus to be to the Southwards of Cape Cod 554

Miles, and to the Westwards 34 Miles. Therefore the Current in that time, namely, in 9 days, hath set to the Northwards 67 Miles, and to the Eastwards 64 Miles; that is North East a little Northerly, 93 miles, which is $10\frac{1}{3}$ Miles every day.

From *Bermudus* to *Cape Cod*

	North.	*South.*	*Eaft.*	*Weft.*
North 20 Miles	20.0			
North North weft 150 Miles	138.6			57.4
North by Weft 180 Miles	176.5			35.2
North 90 Miles	90.0			
North Eaft 88 Miles	62.2		62.2	
528 Miles	487.3		62.2	92.5
				62.2
				30.3

• From the second line of the table you can see that 150 miles in a NNW direction is split into a northerly component of 138.6 miles and a westerly component of 57.4 miles. Use this to find the bearing equivalent to NNW. From the third line, find the meaning of North by West.

• Make a scale drawing of the journey. Show also the journey homewards and the discrepancy caused by the current.

8 Admit that Tulis-stairs bear from Billingsgate-stairs S.W., and be distance $\frac{1}{4}$ mile; and suppose the Tide of Ebb to run there Eastward $2\frac{1}{2}$ Miles an Hour, and that a pair of Oars rowing $4\frac{1}{2}$ miles an Hour, would go straight over from the first to the second: how shall they row over; namely upon what Deg., and in what time?

Surveying the land

Briefing

This is about using and applying mathematics in a practical context. Look at a few of the reasons why people wanted to make maps of the land, and how they set about it.

A seventeenth-century example concerns local mapping, measuring lengths and angles and coping with errors. Practical work yields data which can be handled by scale drawing or sine formula. Consider the range of experimental errors and averaging.

The ambitious national survey around AD 1800 illustrates the drive for accuracy and provides older pupils with work on arc length, use of sine formula and angles given in degrees, minutes and seconds.

Background

Whilst lauding the 'Sciences and Artes Mathematicall' in his Preface of 1570, John Dee[1] named more than thirty branches of mathematics and its applications, running from Anthropographie to Zographie! The theme of this chapter came under the heading 'Geometrie, vulgar: which teacheth Measuring', divided into:

How farre: called Apomecometrie;
How high or deepe: called Hypsometrie;
How broad: called Platometrie;
of which are growen the Feates and Artes of Geodesie: more cunningly to Measure and Survey Landes, Woods, Waters etc.

Other authors coined different names for the subjects of their books. Two examples in this chapter illustrate progress from the seventeenth to the eighteenth century, made possible because of the advancing skill of instrument makers.

William LEYBOURN (or Leybourne) (1626–1716)[2] wrote for practitioners involved in local surveying schemes. He has chapter headings such as 'How a Lordship lying in Common Field is to be inclosed' and 'Concerning bogs and Quagmires'! The demand for surveying of manors was not a mere whim, but related to the major change which took place in the rural scene during the sixteenth and seventeenth centuries. The medieval system of open fields, cultivated in strips by different tenants, gave way to enclosed fields, either arable, meadow (for hay) or pasture.

On the positive side this led to greater efficiency and productivity. On the negative side, there were families who lost rights to land. Then the contentious conversion of ploughed land to grazing for sheep generated wealth for landowners and the wool trade, but put many who had previously tilled the soil out of work. In a succession of Enclosures Acts, we can see some of the social connotations of the surveyor's work.

Leybourn himself was originally a printer, but gradually developed skills as a mathematical practitioner and tutor. From his home in Southall (now Greater London) he advertised:

Early theodolite in use.

If any gentleman, or other person, desire to be instructed in any of the Sciences Mathematicall ... the Author will be ready to attend them at times appointed. Also if any Person would have his Land or any Ground for Building surveyed, or any Edifice or Building measured, either for Carpenters, Bricklayers, Plaisterers ... he is ready to perform the same.

Likewise, he offered sun dials for the garden. He carried out many estate surveys and was involved in the major survey of London following the Great Fire of 1666. As a writer he was prolific. The extracts here come from just two volumes, *The Compleat Surveyor* (4th edition 1679, first published as *Planometria* in 1650) and *Cursus Mathematicus*, a comprehensive volume of nine books published in 1690.

Before Leybourn's time, a surveyor named Christopher Saxton had carried out a county-by-county survey of England and Wales. He produced fine maps during the 1570s which were not superseded for over two hundred years. When a new national survey was eventually undertaken towards the end of the eighteenth century, many people played a part.

A full and fascinating report of the survey was written for the Royal Society by William Mudge (1762–1829),[3] an officer in the Royal Engineers, who directed the work. William's uncle was a clock maker and his father a physician in Plymouth, who also received an award for his work on telescope mirrors. The young Mudge was given a professional mathematics education at the Royal Military Academy, recently founded (1741) at Woolwich.

A highly condensed version of Mudge's report on **sheet 11.4** outlines the story: how General Roy's mapping of Scotland after the battle of Culloden led to plans for a new national survey, how this was delayed on account of the Seven Years War with France and then the American War of Independence, and afterwards how it was linked with a project to establish the precise relationship between the meridians through Greenwich and Paris, important because of the major astronomical observatories in each place. In 1791 the Ordnance Survey Office for this Triangulation was established and the Ordnance Survey has been responsible for British cartography ever since.

Whereas Leybourn reckoned to measure angles to half a degree (30 minutes) or occasionally greater accuracy, Mudge records results, not only to the minute, but to the nearest second of arc ($\frac{1}{3600}$ of a degree). This was possible because of the Great Theodolite, designed and made for the purpose by Jesse Ramsden, see **sheet 11.5**. This wonder of the instrument world had a circular brass scale three feet in diameter, graduated in quarters of a degree. The fine readings were taken by means of two microscopes on opposite sides of the circle. Each microscope was adjusted by a micrometer screw, on the head of which was a scale giving the seconds. On a clear day, with its telescopic sights, the theodolite could be focused on a reference point 70 miles away!

Jesse Ramsden (1735–1800)[4] was the son of a Halifax inn-keeper. He was first apprenticed to a clothier, but then worked with several of the well-known London instrument makers. He set up his own shop, married the sister of another instrument maker, and gradually built up his reputation. The expertise of instrument makers was by then very impressive, but great skill and patience were required for engraving even and accurate scale divisions. Ramsden achieved fame, and a grant of £615 from the Board of Longitude, for inventing a machine which could be used to divide scales to a high degree of accuracy. At one time he employed about sixty workers, and such was the quality of their work that many of the instruments have been preserved to this day. In 1786 he

was elected a Fellow of the Royal Society, and later awarded a medal for his work.

In the classroom

The sheets can be used to support a variety of work at different levels, most effectively done in connection with some practical surveying. If a theodolite is available, then angles can be measured with sufficient accuracy to give reasonable results. Otherwise a crude form of plane tabling can be improvised to give a feeling for the principles.

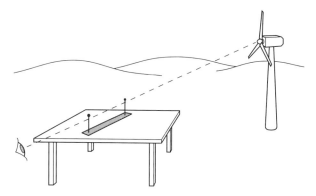

Sighting with a plane table.

Paper is taped to a desk and set as level as possible. A sighting rule consisting of a straight edge with vertical pins fixed at either end is required. This is aligned with a landmark by eye and a pencil line drawn along the straight edge. Without moving the table, a second landmark (or another base station) is sighted and its direction ruled in. The angle between the two lines drawn on the paper is the angle required.

Sheet 11.1 The principle of triangulation

A base line between two stations needs to be measured carefully. Then sightings of prominent objects are taken from each station. A scale drawing is made to pin-point the position of each object; distances can be determined from the drawing. Pupils can do this practically out of doors, or they can take data from Fig. XII on the sheet.

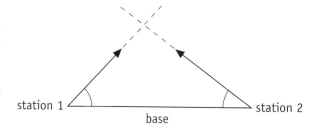

Principle of triangulation.

Ships at anchor. Using the data on the sheet, pupils map the ships' positions. A perch was a rod for measuring land, $5\frac{1}{2}$ yards standard length but varying locally! 5 metres is close to 1 perch length. Pupils should check some of the distances given and measure more of their own.

Error handling. After fieldwork and after scale drawing, compare results from different members of the class. What is the range of measurements? What is the best average to take – mode, median or mean?

Distances by calculation using trigonometry. How far away is the most distant ship? This requires the sine formula. How far apart are the two closest ships? This requires the cosine formula.

Sheet 11.2 Three ways of surveying a field

Test drawing skill. Pupils plot the fields from data given on the sheet (methods 1 and 3). If the lines do not close when they come to the last edge of the field, then there is an error which needs to be traced.

Engage pupils in weighing up the pros and cons of each method (and comparing them with any other methods such as offset surveys which they may know about). There will be considerations both of economy, such as the number of measurements to be made and the amount of walking involved, and of how best to be accurate.

Plan a practical project. Pupils identify potential sources of error and decide on reasonable precautions. Experimental results are always approximate, and it is useful to know the likely range of error.

Sheet 11.3

Sheet 11.3 is intended as a poster to encourage care in the presentation of projects. A muller is a stone for pounding or grinding on the grinding slab.

Sheets 11.4 to 11.7 The great triangulation survey of Britain under George III and the founding of the Ordnance Survey

Read the account. Pupils can consider what conditions are necessary for a mapping enterprise of this magnitude. Their list may include peace, funds, official interest, experienced surveyors and a disciplined team, highly skilled instrument makers and reasonable roads.

On the diagram pupils can identify the parts of the theodolite described in the text, estimate its assembled height, and then estimate the size in millimetres of each scale division, knowing the diameter.

Relate the angles taken to the map. Using sheets 11.6 and 11.7, members of the class can select a triangle each and fill in its angles. Do the angles add to $180°0'0''$? If not, what is the percentage error?

To get an idea of the implication of a small error in angle, pupils can work out the distance between two points subtending an angle of 1 second at a distance of 20 miles (answer about 15 cm). In taking the angles, measurements were normally repeated two or three times, but on sheet 11.6 only the mean is given, except for the crucial bases of Old Sarum and Beacon Hill.

To get a feel for the way knowledge of distance and position was built up, pupils may start from the 36 600 ft base of 1794. Using the sine formula in successive triangles, calculate the distance from Beacon Hill to Dean Hill. The shortest method is via Four Mile Stone, but a check is provided by working via Thorney Down and Highclere. Thus the potential build-up of errors was minimized.

Further information. The line of the meridian at Dunnose was determined independently by astronomical sightings. The survey proceeded along the crucial south coast and then slowly through the rest of the country. After the main triangles, interior triangles were established with a smaller theodolite and detailed surveying carried out to produce maps on the scale of 1 inch to 1 mile. By mid-century even greater detail was required for the planning of railways.

William Leybourn suggests use of a theodolite

As the quadrant was the most convenient Instrument for the taking of Altitudes, so the Theodolite is the best for taking of Distances of Trees, Steeples, Towers etc., either of one or of many together.

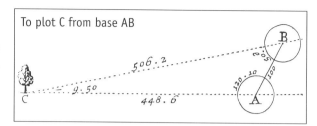

To plot C from base AB

Suppofing that A B C D E and F were a Squadron of Ships lying at Anchor, and you being on fhore, and defirous to make a Draught of them, reprefenting their Situation and true Diftance one from another.

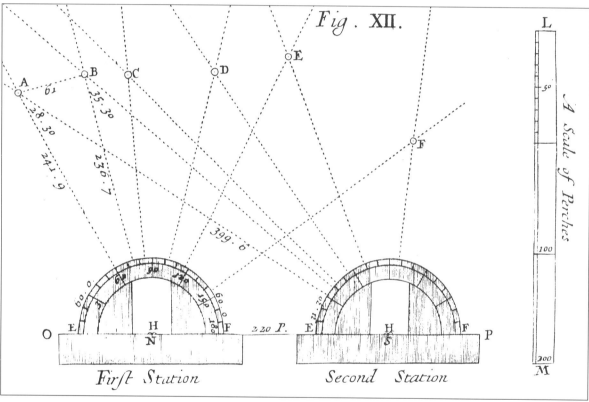

Fig. XII.

Firft Station   *Second Station*

A Scale of Perches

Seek out two convenient places upon the fhore.

	At the first station the Index Cut		**Stationary Distance 220 perches**	At the second station the Index Cut		
	De	M		De	M	
A	60	00		31	30	A
B	74	30		38	40	B
C	84	30		43	20	C
D	104	50		54	00	D
E	117	00		68	10	E
F	145	10		97	00	F

Upon a Sheet of large Paper or Parchment, lay down the obfervations taken.

Three ways of surveying a field in MDCXC

It moft commonly happeneth, when a Lordfhip is to be improved wherein are many Free-holders, that their ground lies for the most part difperfed, and intermixt one amongft another in all parts and quarters of the Field. Therefore to find the juft Quantity of every man's ground, the Surveyour is to prepare a Field-book ...

William LEYBOURN (1626–1716)

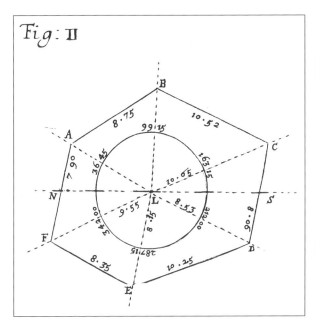

Fig: II

1 How to take the plot of a fmall Inclofure at one Station.

	Deg.	Min.	Chains	Links
A	36	45	7	90
B	99	15	8	75
C	163	15	10	52
D	212	00	8	6
E	287	15	10	25
F	342	00	8	35

2 How to take the Plot of a field at Two Stations, taken in any Two Places thereof, from either of which all the angles in the field may be feen, and by meafuring only the Stationary Diftance.

This is similar to the ships at anchor, sheet 11.1.

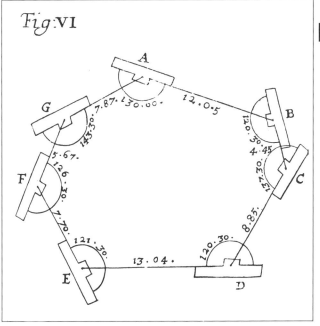

Fig:VI

3 How to take the Plot of a Wood, Park or other large Champain plain by going around about the fame and making obfervation at every angle thereof.

This way of surveying, (which is inferior to none, although not altogether so expeditious as some ways) hath a preheminence above the rest, for by help of your Field Book you may (before you go out of the Field) know whether your Plot will close at the end of your Protraction:

Collect the quantity of all the Angles found at your several Observations into one sum, and multiply 180 degrees by a number less by two than the number of Angles in the Field: and if the product of this multiplication be equal to the total sum of your Angles, then is your work true, otherwise not.

• Apply this test to the example shown in Fig. VI.

11.3

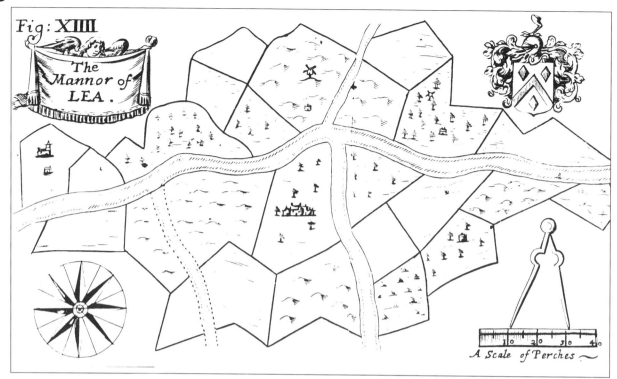

The Names of such Colours as are necessary for the Washing of Maps, Plots, or Charts.

REDS	YELLOWS	BLEWS	GREENES
Vermilion	Gumbooge	Bice	Bice
Lake	Yellow Berries	Indigo	Sap Green
Red Lead	Orpiment, *i.e.*	Verditer	Vertdegriece
Roffet	Arfnick	Litmofe	Verditure.
Brazeel	Mafticot.	Logwood.	
Turnfoil			
Indian Cakes.			

BLACKS	WHITES	BROWNS
Lamp black	White Lead in	Spanifh Brown
Printers Black	flakes	Umber
Ivory ⎫Shavings		Wood Soot
Hartfhorn ⎰burnt.		Rindes of green
		Wall-nuts.

Being thus provided of thefe feverall Colours here named, which you may have in divers places in *London*, as alfo of a Grinding-ftone and Muller, which any Mafon in *London* will furnifh you with, alfo divers Pencils of feverall fizes, and Gally-pots, Gar-Glaffes, or Horfe-Mufcle-fhells, to put your Colours in when they are ground and tempered, you are then ready at any time to make ufe of them. And now will I fhew you how all the fore-mentioned Colours are to be ground and tempered.

Account of the Trigonometrical Survey

(highly condensed)

Introduction. Accurate surveys of a country are universally admitted to be works of great public utility, as affording the surest foundation for almost every kind of internal improvement in time of peace, and the best means of forming judicious plans of defence against the invasions of an enemy in time of war.

The rise and progress of the rebellion which broke out in the Highlands of Scotland in 1745, convinced Government of what infinite importance it would be to the State, that a country, so very inaccessible by nature, should be thoroughly explored and laid open. My friend conceived the idea of making a map, but the breaking out of the war of 1755 prevented its completion.

On the conclusion of the peace of 1763, it came for the first time under the consideration of Government, to make a general Survey of the whole Island at the public cost … the nation's being unfortunately involved in the American war …

The peace of 1783 being concluded, in the beginning of October, Comte d'Ademar, the French Ambassador, transmitted to Mr. Fox, then one of His Majesty's principal Secretaries of State, a Memoir of M. Cassini de Thury, in which he sets forth the great advantage that would accrue to astronomy, by carrying a series of triangles from the neighbourhood of London to Dover, there to be connected with those already executed in France, by which combined operations the relative situations of the two most famous observatories in Europe, Greenwich and Paris, would be more accurately ascertained than they are at present.

A generous and beneficent Monarch, whose knowledge and love of the sciences are sufficiently evinced by the protection which HE constantly affords them, and under whose auspices they are seen daily to flourish, soon supplied the funds that were judged necessary.

Choice of the Base. Hounslow Heath appeared to be the most eligible situation because of its vicinity to the Capital and the Royal Observatory at Greenwich, its great extent, and the extraordinary levelness of its surface, without any local obstructions.

The first part of the operation would be the clearing from furze bushes and ant hills of a narrow tract along the heath. It was judged right to obtain and employ soldiers, instead of country labourers. Accordingly, a party consisting of a serjeant, corporal, and 10 men, were ordered to march from Windsor to Hounslow Heath, where they encamped on 26th of May 1784. Owing to the extraordinary wetness of the season, this operation required more time than had been at first imagined. We shall therefore leave it going on, and in the mean time proceed to describe the instruments that were used.

Steel Chain. One of the first instruments, which that able artist Mr. Ramsden had orders to prepare, was a steel chain, one hundred feet in length, the best that he could make. It was hoped that an instrument of this sort might be made, which would measure distances much more accurately than any thing of that kind had ever done before. The measurement of bases has always been found to be tedious and troublesome, uncertain likewise when done with rods of deal.

Instrument with which the Angles were observed. It is a brass circle, three feet in diameter, and may be called a great Theodolite, rendered extremely perfect. The circle is attached by ten conical tubes, as so many radii, to a large vertical, conical hollow axis, called the exterior axis. The instrument rests on three feet upon which rises a vertical hollow cone called the interior axis. Thus the circle being lifted up by two men laying hold of its radii, and the exterior being placed upon the interior axis, it turns round very smoothly, and free from any central shake. This mode of centering is one of the chief excellencies of the instrument.

Two achromatic telescopes, with double object-glasses of two inches and a half aperture, belong to the instrument. The instrument has two very good spirit levels, that are fitted with several means of adjustment.

Two vertical microscopes are used for reading off the divisions on the opposite sides of the circle immediately under them. Now it will easily be conceived how readily, as well as accurately, any observation of an angle can be read off with such an instrument; for the degrees and quarters, that is to say, the 15′, 30′, or 45′, being seen with the naked eye and registered, the value of the fractional space between zero and the last grand division seen in the field of the microscope is obtained by turning the micrometer head until the moveable wire bisects the dot at that grand division.

The instrument weighed in the whole about 200 lbs. It is contained in two deal boxes. The whole attirail,* including stand, steps, stools, pullies, ropes, tent etc., was transported from place to place in a four wheeled spring carriage, drawn by two, and sometimes by four horses.

* apparatus, gear.

Ramsden's Great Theodolite

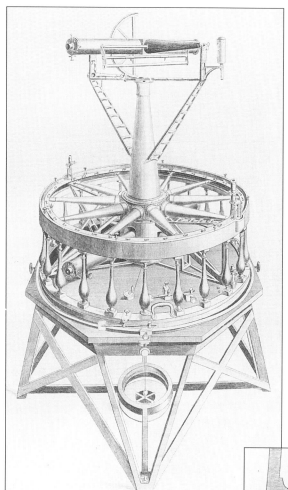

General view

Plan

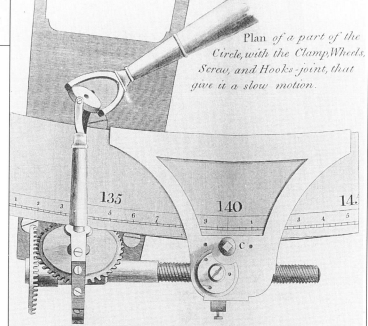

Part of the circle

Angles taken in the Trigonometrical Survey

1792 at Butser Hill

Between	Deg.	Min.	Sec.
Rook's Hill and Hind Head	70	25	13.75
Rook's Hill and Dunnose	80	21	58
Rook's Hill and Motteston Down	101	7	8
Rook's Hill and Highclere	154	56	57.25
Rook's Hill and Dean Hill (dubious)	156	34	14

Angles taken in the Year 1793

(excluding Chancontbury Ring and Ditchling Beacon)

At Motteston Down

Between	°	′	Mean ″
Nine Barrow Down and Dunnose	159	51	3.75
Butser Hill and Dunnose	64	41	2

At Dunnose

Between	°	′	Mean ″
Dean Hill and Brading staff	55	58	38.5
Motteston Down and Brading staff	94	49	19
Nine Barrow Down and Brading staff	109	11	5.75
Butser Hill and Brading staff	0	15	31.5

At Dean Hill

Between	°	′	Mean ″
Beacon Hill and Highclere	50	18	47.5
Beacon Hill and Wingreen	82	56	48.5
Beacon Hill and Dunnose	160	46	8.5
Beacon Hill and Nine Barrow Down	134	23	32.5
Beacon Hill and Motteston Down	174	34	57.5
Beacon Hill and Four Mile Stone	39	29	3.25
Beacon Hill and Butser Hill	112	41	36.75

At Old Sarum

Between	°	′	″
Beacon Hill and Four Mile Stone	85	58	{ 21.5 / 21.75 / 22.25 / 23.75 }
mean number of seconds 22.25			
Beacon Hill and Thorney Down	48	26	{ 3 / 4.25 / 6.5 }
mean number of seconds 4.5			

At Four Mile Stone

Between	°	′	Mean ″
Beacon Hill and Old Sarum	70	1	47.5
Beacon Hill and Dean Hill	72	4	48

At Beacon Hill

Between	°	′	″
Old Sarum and Four Mile Stone	23	59	{ 50.25 / 52.25 }
mean number of seconds 51.25			
Old Sarum and Thorney Down	33	33	{ 23.75 / 24 / 26 }
mean number of seconds 24.5			
Dean Hill and Four Mile Stone	68	26	{ 8.5 / 10.5 / 11 }
mean number of seconds 10			
Dean Hill and Highclere	102	45	23.5
Thorney Down and Highclere	113	38	{ 13.75 / 16.75 }
mean number of seconds 15.25			

At Thorney Down

Between	°	′	Mean ″
Beacon Hill and Highclere	53	22	29.25
Beacon Hill and Old Sarum	98	0	31

At Highclere

Between	°	′	Mean ″
Dean Hill and Beacon Hill	26	55	53.5

Owing to a strain which the clamp sustained when at Thorney Down, no dependence can be placed on this observation and, the season being far advanced, the party returned to London.

Operations of the Year 1794

The party took the field the fourth of March, and proceeded from London to the Isle of Purbeck, taking Butser Hill in its way.

It was necessary to start so early in order to finish measuring the base on Salisbury Plain before the ground to the northward of Old Sarum would be ploughed.

Angles taken in the Year 1794

(those relevant to sheet 11.7)

At Butser Hill

Between	°	′	Mean ″
Rook's Hill and Dean Hill	156	34	20

At Nine Barrow Down

Between	°	′	Mean ″
Dean Hill and Wingreen	39	34	28.75
Dean Hill and Motteston Down	56	9	55.25
Dean Hill and Dunnose	61	57	20

At Wingreen

Between	°	′	Mean ″
Beacon Hill and Dean Hill	30	13	23
Dean Hill and Nine Barrow Down	88	58	46.5

At Highclere

Between	°	′	Mean ″
Butser Hill and Dean Hill	69	8	35
Dean Hill and Beacon Hill	26	55	51.5
Thorney Down and Beacon Hill	12	59	10

At Beacon Hill

Between	°	′	Mean ″
Dean Hill and Wingreen	66	49	52

Situations of the Stations

Dean Hill, Hampshire.
This place is near the village of Dean: the station is in the north-west corner of a field belonging to Mr. Haliday.

Highclere, Wiltshire.
The station is the centre of the Ring on Beacon Hill.

Hind Head, Surrey.
The station is near the Gibbet, being about 22 feet north-west of it.

etc.

Plan of the principal triangles

(from Butser Hill to the West)
in the Trigonometrical Survey
MDCCXCI–MDCCXCIV

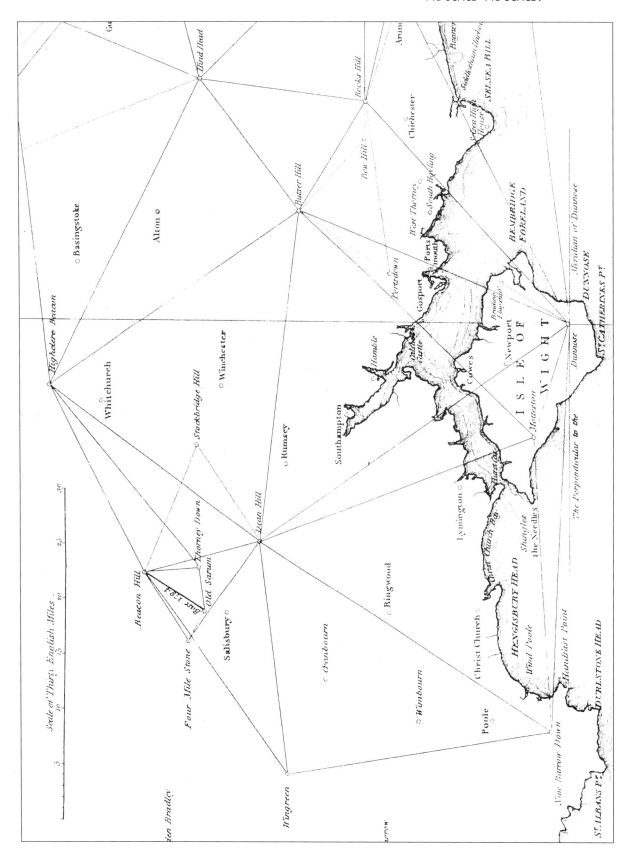

The *Ladies' Diary*

Briefing

Recreational mathematics began to appear in English journals and newspapers during the first half of the eighteenth century, providing opportunities for people previously excluded to engage in mathematical problem solving. For one woman at the beginning of the nineteenth century, we know that it was a step on her difficult road to scientific achievement.

The sheets give examples of puzzles at different levels, requiring in the first place easy algebra, then harder mensuration, and finally some elementary mechanics. You can include social comment and discussion at any level.

Background

As the printing of books opened up opportunities for learning during the sixteenth century, so the development of newspapers and periodicals at the turn of the eighteenth century widened the scope still further. The *Ladies' Diary* or *Woman's Almanack* was an annual publication, launched in 1704.

Almanacs had been popular for a long time. Normally they were part reference book, part astrology. To tables such as those giving the moon's phases and the times of the rising and setting of the sun would be added dates of events like fairs, and then medical and farming advice based on astrology, giving the most fortunate time to sow, to breed and kill livestock, to fell timber and so on. There were often predictions about plague, crime, weather, the progress of wars and other matters of common concern.

By the eighteenth century, there was less commitment to astrology: indeed the *Ladies' Diary* declared 'there is no such thing as foretelling events'.[1] It contained the usual astronomical and special events data plus articles similar to a women's magazine of today with a section of riddles or 'enigmas'. This section was very successful and, over the years, the *Diary* gained a particular reputation for its mathematical puzzles. Solutions sent in by readers were published the following year, and prizes (normally some free copies of the *Diary*) were awarded for certain problems.

The mathematical demands of the problems varied from quite easy to hard. Similarly the *Diary* attracted a wide range of contributors, from the unknown to the eminent. In the *Edinburgh Review* of 1808,[2] we find discussed:

the inferiority [in the higher department] of English mathematicians since the time of Newton [but] ... it is but fair to acknowledge, that a certain degree of mathematical science, and indeed no inconsiderable degree, is perhaps more widely diffused in England than in any other country of the world. The Ladies' Diary, with several other periodical and popular publications of the same kind, are the best proofs of this assertion. In these, many curious problems, not of the highest order indeed, but still having a considerable degree of difficulty, and far beyond the mere elements of science, are often to be met with: and the great number of ingenious men who take a share in proposing, and answering these questions, whom one has never heard of anywhere else, is not a little surprising. Nothing of the same kind, we believe, is to be found in any other country ... If there is a decline, therefore, or a deficiency in mathematical knowledge in this country, it is not to the genius of the people, but to some other cause, that it must be attributed.

It may appear from this that the contributors were male! However, women did share in the proposing and answering of questions. There were only a few, but numbers are perhaps less significant than the fact that there were any at all.

The obstacles to women's participation in the sciences were still formidable at this time. Young women who showed a serious interest, the beginnings of talent, were liable to be discouraged on the grounds that it would strain their health! Whilst an educated and leisured middle class of women was emerging, for them scientific study beyond the basics would be unusual and socially questionable.

We are all constrained in various ways by the expectations of society, but the demarcation of interests considered seemly for a women was far stronger then than the vestiges which remain today. For instance, Mary SOMERVILLE (1780–1872), one of the first to become a scientist in her own right, recounts how she became aware of algebra during her early teens:

I was often invited with my mother to tea parties ... which bored me exceedingly, but I became acquainted with a Miss Ogilvie, much younger than the rest, who ... showed me a monthly magazine with coloured plates of ladies' dresses, charades, and puzzles. At the end of a page I read what appeared to me to be simply an arithmetical question; but on turning the page I was surprised to see strange looking lines mixed with letters, chiefly X's and Y's, and asked; 'What is that?' 'Oh,' said Miss Ogilvie, 'it is a kind of arithmetic: they call it Algebra; but I can tell you nothing about it.'[3]

Mary looked in vain amongst the books at home for enlightenment, but was unable to ask anyone, 'for I should have been laughed at', and, 'as to going to a bookseller ... the thing was impossible! ... so no more could be done at that time; but I never lost sight of an object which had interested me from the first.' Later she persuaded her brother's tutor to buy the books she needed.

The *Ladies' Diary* and other periodicals were more accessible. After her marriage, the birth of two sons, and widowhood, Mary frequently tackled the problems in another journal, the *Mathematical Repository*. She writes: 'At last [in 1811] I succeeded in solving a prize problem! ... and I was awarded a silver medal cast on purpose with my name, which pleased me exceedingly.'

At this time, the need for female higher education was just beginning to be debated, at least amongst Edinburgh intellectuals. Clearly the possibility of women's participation through this sort of journal was very important in demonstrating their ability and interest, perhaps in building confidence and establishing contacts. This certainly happened for Mary Somerville and, with the encouragement of her second husband, led on to original experiments with solar rays and writings in physical science.

Returning to the early days of the *Diary*, 1704, we find that the idea of mathematics for recreation was not new, but it had been given a new lease of life by the exciting climate of scientific discovery and philosophical debate. Presumably such considerations led the first editor, a Coventry schoolteacher, to believe that mathematical puzzles would be a success in this journal, primarily intended 'for the Use and Diversion of the FAIR-SEX'.

In today's environment it is difficult to imagine the impact made on popular consciousness by a scientific explanation of the rainbow (for instance) – its colours and the reason why it appears when sun and rain occur together. Previously the rainbow was considered a sign from God, who said to Noah, 'I do set my bow in the cloud, and it shall be for a token ...'.[4] The boldness of natural philosophy was as much a subject of conversation as politics and social news. Contemporary poets joined the debate: in 'An Essay on Man' (1733), Alexander Pope, somewhat sceptically, wrote:

Go, wond'rous creature! mount where Science guides,
Go, measure earth, weigh air, and state the tides;
Instruct the planets in what orbs to run,
Correct old Time, and regulate the Sun;
...
Go, teach Eternal Wisdom how to rule –
Then drop into thyself, and be a fool!

Women of the middle and upper classes were not alone in benefiting from the atmosphere of intellectual enquiry and curiosity about the world at large.

Mary Somerville (1780–1872).

By 1700, a London news sheet could be bought for one half-penny by the 'poorer sort of people'. Then as printers were released from the limitations of the Licensing Acts, provincial newspapers came into being, as did colonial papers such as the *Boston News Letter*. Reading was no longer quite so confined to the few, and a newspaper had to consider not only traditional readers, such as gentry, clergy and town merchants, but also farmers, shopkeepers, artisans and labourers.

Particularly in the peaceful interludes between wars, news was supplemented with material to entertain and instruct. For instance, in 1739, the *Newcastle Journal* began a series of essays on such topics as the Gulf Stream, and the *Leeds Mercury* introduced puzzles posed and answered by readers. The *Derby Mercury* started to include mathematical problems. Throughout the country it began to be possible for ordinary people to learn the basic skills of reading and 'cyphering' at village schools and then to exercise those skills through the newspaper.[5]

A newspaper of those days was not just read quickly and then thrown away. Often it was the only printed matter that was available to its readers, and was something to be read and re-read by many people, discussed and argued over, and finally carefully preserved. It is interesting that in the very different circumstances of today, puzzle features are still to be found in many papers.

In the classroom

Any of these sheets can be related to discussion of educational opportunities and/or the media.

This is recreational mathematics, but offers an opportunity to raise awareness of how very recently we have come to expect education for all, and of how access to reading material is an aid to emancipation.

Sheet 12.1 Hidden ages
Can pupils get the meaning of the verse?
(A score means 20.)
Answer: $A + A/2 + A/3 + 3 \times 3 = 6 \times 20 + 10$,
        so my age is 66 years.
Check: $66 + 33 + 22 + 9 = 130$.
Pupils can try some of the other questions. Other activities for pupils could include:

Hide your own (or a friend's or relative's) age in a puzzle.

Collect mathematical problems from newspapers and magazines; sort, discuss, display and try some.

Sheet 12.2 Kettles and cones
These are more demanding brain teasers.

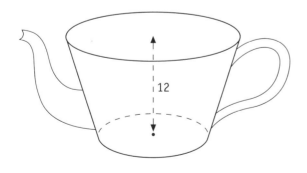

Ask pupils to describe the kettle in their own words, and to draw and label it.

Its shape is the frustum of a cone with, say, upper diameter 5*k* and lower diameter 3*k*. Given that the depth of the kettle is 12 inches, what would be the depth of the whole cone from which the shape is taken?

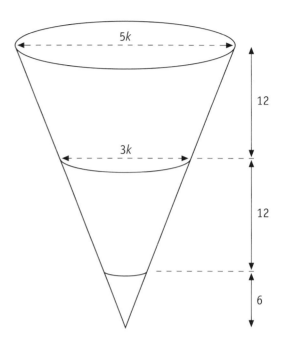

Going down 12 reduces the diameter from 5*k* to 3*k*, down another 12 would reduce to 1*k* and another 6 reduce the diameter to zero. Therefore the depth of the whole cone is 30 inches. Using the formula $\frac{1}{3}\pi r^2 h$ for the volume of a cone, the volume of the kettle is:

$$\tfrac{1}{3}\pi \left(\frac{5k}{2} \right)^2 \times 30 - \tfrac{1}{3}\pi \left(\frac{3k}{2} \right)^2 \times 18$$

This is the volume in cubic inches. If the kettle is to hold 13 gallons, the volume must be equal to 13×282 cubic inches. Hence $k = 4.88$.

The diameters of the top and bottom of the kettle are therefore 24.40 inches and 14.64 inches.

An interesting alternative method is given by a later editor. He uses a formula, known in ancient China,[6] and analogous to the one for the frustum of a pyramid explored on sheets 7.3 and 7.4. Your pupils might like to guess at the frustum of a cone formula on the basis of this analogy, and then make a check.

Sheet 12.3 Vibrations and free fall
Using the title page of the *Diary*, pupils might:

Deduce the year of first publication, given that the *Diary* was issued annually.

Comment on other information presented in this title page.

Research the reign of Queen Anne.

Consider why problems on the pendulum, sound and falling bodies might have been popular or newsworthy at that time (see below).

The selection of problems – pendulum, free fall and speed of sound – was topical in several ways. Pendulum clocks were relatively new. The first commercial model was designed by Christian Huygens and constructed at The Hague in 1657. It immediately produced a great improvement in the accuracy of timekeeping. English clockmakers rapidly developed the technology, both for the traditional table clock and for the new design of the longcase or grandfather clock. The esteem of these early clockmakers can be judged by the memorial in Westminster Abbey to Thomas Tompion (perhaps the most famous), who died in 1713.

The pendulum was also in the news on account of a lively debate about the shape of the earth. At the equator, a pendulum of given length vibrates slower than in more northerly (or southerly) latitudes. According to Newton, this meant that the earth is not a perfect sphere but is flattened at the poles. Others argued the opposite, and measuring expeditions were eventually sent as far afield as Peru and Lapland to resolve the question.

Newton had also worked out a theoretical value for the velocity of sound in dry air which differed somewhat from the results of various experiments which were being carried out at about this time. The discrepancy was later to be resolved by Laplace.

Clock by Thomas Tompion, London, *c.* 1680.

Hidden ages

1707   **Question** from the *Ladies' Diary*

> If to my age there added be
> Its half, its third, and three times three;
> Six score and ten the sum you'd see,
> Pray find out what my age may be.

The *Ladies' Diary* soon became famous for its mathematical puzzles. At first even the solutions had to be in rhyme, but that idea was soon dropped!
You can see it was popular with men as well as women:

1712   **Question** by Mr. John Wilson

> A person being asked his age replied, if to the months of my age you add their one half and one eighth, the sum will be 442: What was his age?
>
> *Answered by* Mrs. Mary Nelson

1713   **Question** by Mrs. Sarah Brown

> A lady being warmly importuned by her lover to consent to their union, answered, that she thought herself then too young: the lover desired to be informed when she would think herself old enough to make him happy; she replied, when the square of her age diminished by $\frac{1}{3}$ and then increased by $\frac{1}{9}$ of the same was 891: What would then be her age?
>
> *Answered by* Mr. Lingen from Ireland

- Now try these puzzles from the twentieth century, and make up one of your own:

1917

Rover was asleep on the rug when a visitor asked his age.

'Well, five years ago,' said Mary, 'my brother was five times as old as the dog, but now he is only three times as old.'

■ *Can you tell Rover's age?*

1935

I met Mrs. Calculus in the bank with a pile of notes.

'You see this money,' she said, 'whilst the chidren are all at school, I am going to invest it for them.'

'Very nice too,' said I, 'but why that particular amount?'

'I'm working to a formula, you'll never guess what it is.'

I thought for a moment. 'Yes, I know, you've added up their ages (in years) and then squared the total.'

'Well no,' she said, 'I didn't do it that way. I took Alice's age, added the square of Brian's age and the cube of Clare's age. The total is exactly the number of pounds I have here.'

■ *What are the ages of the three children?*

Kettles and cones

A question from the *Ladies' Diary* of 1711:

> I happen'd one ev'ning with a tinker to sit,
> Whose tongue ran a great deal too fast for his wit:
> He talk'd of his art with abundance of mettle,
> So I ask'd him to make me a flat-bottomed kettle,
> That the top and the bottom diameters be
> In just such proportion as five is to three.
> Twelve inches the depth I would have and no more,
> And to hold in ale gallons seven less than a score.
> He promis'd to do't, and to work he strait went;
> But when he had done it he found it too scant.
> He alter'd it then and too big he had made it,
> And when it held right the diameters fail'd it:
> So that making't so often, too big or too little,
> The tinker at last had quite spoil'd the kettle:
> Yet he vows he will bring his said purpose to pass,
> Or he'll utterly spoil ev'ry ounce of his brass.
> To prevent him from ruin, I pray help him out,
> The diameter's length else he'll never find out.

(You will need to know that 282 cubic inches make a gallon.)

The ingenious Mrs. Barbara Sidway, in her answer to this question, proposed another very pretty question:

> If the kettle was to hold as much again by adding to the wider end, what would be the depth of the part added?

(Suppose the whole kettle to remain in the form of a frustum of a cone.)

Another question proposed by Mrs. Barbara Sidway in 1711:

> From a given cone to cut the greatest cylinder possible.

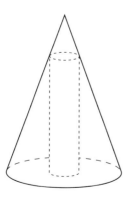 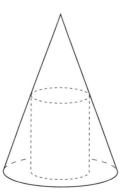 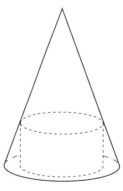 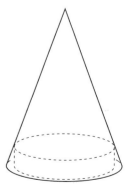

12.3

Vibrations and free fall

Topical problems from the reign of Queen Anne

Question proposed in 1709:

What is the length of the pendulum which will make as many vibrations in a minute as it is inches in length?

(A seconds pendulum is 39.2 inches.)

Question proposed in 1713:

In what time would a heavy body fall freely from a height of seven miles to the surface of the earth, the force of gravity being supposed uniform, and no resistance from the air, also in what time would sound move to the same height?

Answered by Mr. John Newbold and Mrs. Mary Nelson.

Mrs. Sidway also answered this question, and at the same time proposed the following one:

From what height must a heavy body fall so that the time of descent to the earth's surface may be equal to the time in which sound would move to the same height; and with what velocity would the body strike the ground?

(The velocity of sound varies according to temperature and other conditions; take it to be approximately 740 miles per hour or 331 metres/second. There are 1609 metres to a mile, and gravity causes an acceleration of approximately 9.81 metres/second[2].)

> **And to a-uoide the tedioufe repetition of thefe woozdes : is e-qualle to : I will fette as I doe often in woozke bfe, a paire of paralleles, oz Gemowe lines of one lengthe, thus:========, bicaufe noe.2. thynges, can be moare equalle. And now marke thefe noinbers.**
>
> 1. $14.ze.$ ─┼─ $.15.q$ ====== $71.q.$
>
> 2. $20.ze.$ ─────── $.18.q$ ==== $.102.q.$
>
> 3. $26.z$ ─┼─ $10ze$ ==== $9.z$ ─── $10ze$ ─┼─ $213.q.$
>
> 4. $19.ze$ ─┼─ $192.q$ ==== $10z$ ─┼─ $108q$ ─── $19ze$
>
> 5. $18.ze$ ─┼─ $24.q.$ ==== $8.z.$ ─┼─ $2.ze.$
>
> 6. $34z$ ─── $12ze$ ─── ==== $40ze$ ─┼─ $480q$ ─── $9.z$

- You might like to carry out the task of simplifying the equations, using either Recorde's or modern notation.

This facsimile shows the 'equals' sign as it first appeared in print. The book was *The Whetstone of Witte* by Robert Recorde, who says:

> *And to avoid the tedious repetition of these words: is equal to : I will set as I do often in work use, a pair of parallels, or Gemowe lines (twin lines as in Gemini) of one length, thus: ======, because no 2 things, can be more equal.*

When this was published in 1557, symbolic algebra was in the devlopment phase. Authors were busily inventing their own notations, but most commonly for 'equals' they wrote the Latin word 'aequales' or 'aeq.'. Recorde would not want to do that in an English textbook; he was very keen to promote a vocabulary of English words for expressing mathematical ideas.

The Gemowe lines did not catch on immediately, but in 1631 three influential books, one by Harriot, one by Oughtred, and Norwood's *Trigonometria*, were published, all using this sign. Then Newton and other leading English mathematicians used it. Eventually, as we know, it achieved a remarkable worldwide acceptance.

It is interesting to observe the context. The six equations listed are used as exemplars for what we should call 'collecting like terms'. By the variety of signs, you might think there were several unknowns, but that is not the case. This again is a feature of algebra in transition. In a sense the numbers, roots, squares and cubes were thought of as separate entities, whereas we would talk about different powers of one unknown (or root).

		(In our terms)
$\mathcal{Q}$	Betokeneth nomber absolute	constants
$\mathcal{Z}e$	Signifieth the roote of any nomber	x
$\mathcal{Z}$	Representeth a square nomber	x^2
$\mathcal{C}$	Expresseth a Cubike nomber, etc.	x^3

Calculating with chance

Briefing

Study the Pascal–Fermat letters which established the basics of probability theory in 1654. See the theory applied to life expectancies by Abraham de Moivre 84 years later.

Students of 16+ should enjoy the problems and be able to follow the reasoning, either as part of their general education or to consolidate parts of a course on probability.

Background

We take the idea of measuring chance very lightly today, but it is interesting to observe how late in the history of mathematics a theory was developed.[1] The originators, Pascal and Fermat, were two very different characters, and it was left to a third, Christiaan Huygens, to publish a book *On Reasoning in Games of Dice*, which remained the principal introductory text for fifty-years. It is worth noting that Cardan's experience with dice had led him to develop promising ideas on probability a century earlier than this, but his notes on the subject remained unpublished until 1663 and made little impact.

Blaise PASCAL (1623–1662). His mother died when he was three. His own relatively short life was plagued by bouts of illness, but his flair for mathematics was clear from early childhood. His caring father moved the family to Paris. There, in his teens, Pascal was caught up with the enterprising scientific group organized by a friar called Marin Mersenne. Pascal began to write original papers, invented a mechanical calculating machine and became interested in experiments with air pressure and the vacuum. In his twenties he turned sternly religious, only occasionally returning to mathematics.

One of these occasions was in 1654 when it is said that Chevalier de Méré posed to him a gambler's dilemma. Pascal became interested and wrote to Fermat, who was well known for his sharpness in problem solving. Over a period of four months the two of them worked out a clear way of thinking about the odds in dice games. Pascal also wrote about how to apply the arithmetical triangle in these cases, for instance to work out numbers of combinations. Although it was not his invention, the triangle has commonly been known by his name since that time.

Pierre de FERMAT (1601–1665) led a very different life, taking up mathematics as a spare-time interest in his thirties. He was trained in law, married a counsellor's daughter and was himself a counsellor for the parliament of Toulouse. He lived modestly at Toulouse, rarely travelling from the town where he was born. It is told that he caught the plague, was reported dead by a friend, but actually survived and was promoted to be King's Counsellor – still at Toulouse. Fermat is renowned for his work on the properties of primes and other numbers. In some of the letters to Pascal, he even seems to dismiss the gaming problems quite quickly in order to write enthusiastically about his latest discoveries in number theory. He produced no books, but a collection of his papers and letters was published in 1679 by the eldest of his five children, Samuel.

Abraham DE MOIVRE (1667–1754) was born and educated in France. When the Edict of Nantes, protecting Protestants, was revoked, he emigrated to England. After meeting Dr Halley, then assistant secretary of the Royal Society, he became known and respected in scientific circles, but he never managed to obtain a well-paid post. He used to complain about the time he had to spend walking to the different houses where he acted as tutor. In his early days as a refugee, he cut out pages from a volume of Newton's *Principia* in order to study them on these journeys! Later, Newton used to meet him at a coffee shop in London and was reputed to say to earnest students, 'Go to Mr de Moivre, he knows these things better than I do.'

On the continent, Jacques Bernoulli and others were publishing new work on probability, but de Moivre's *Doctrine of Chances* (first edition 1718) was the leading English text. It contained a very clear exposition and several original ideas. In the second edition (1738), de Moivre developed the serious application of probability to finance – such matters as annuities and life insurance.

Governments found the sale of annuities a convenient way to raise revenue, but since for many years in Britain the age of the purchaser was ignored, they may well have lost money in the long run! De Moivre showed clearly how a reasonable estimate of life expectancy could be made, and interest on capital taken into account. His friend, Edmond Halley, had collected statistics on births and deaths, again a novel idea. Although these related only to a five-year period in one city, they did provide some basis for actuarial calculations.

De Moivre continued to publish work on various branches of mathematics throughout his long life. In old age he slept a great deal and reputedly died from 'somnolence' aged eighty-seven.

In the classroom

Some arguments corrected

I like to start with one of the notables who missed the point! Luca Pacioli (1445–1514) was a friar and teacher. He was one of the first to write a book on practical applications of mathematics in the Italian language. As this rolled from the new printing presses in 1494, it became widely known and used. One of his problems was about a fair game (of balla):

> *The players A and B agree to continue until one has won six rounds. The game actually stops when A has won five and B three. How should the stakes be divided?*[2]

Pacioli argues that they should divide the money 5:3. Can students produce an argument to convince him of his error?

Tartaglia gave a different wrong answer! However, he correctly refuted Pacioli by pointing out that if you used the same argument when A had won only one game and B none, you would have to divide the stakes in the ratio 1:0, which is clearly unfair.

Students should draw a tree diagram for the next three throws and show why a fairer division in Pacioli's problem would be 7:1 (see below).

Sheets 12.1, 12.2 and 12.3
The famous correspondence

Problems like Pacioli's were 'in the air' for the next century and a half before Pascal and Fermat resolved them in a generally acceptable way. The extracts are drastically abridged, but hopefully retain a flavour of the originals. Note that a *pistole* or *pistolet* was a gold coin, often specifically at this time a Spanish coin worth somewhat less than an English pound.

Help students to work on the letters by posing specific questions, such as:

1 Pascal's July letter concentrates on a two-player game. Write him a reply giving your own reasoning about this problem.

2 By August/September they were embroiled in a three-player problem. Try to state the question in your own words.

3 How did Pascal misinterpret Fermat at first?

4 Gilles Persone de Roberval was professor of mathematics at Paris. What objection did he make?

5 Mark the table of 27 combinations to show correctly which outcome is favourable to each player. What was the answer on which Pascal and Fermat eventually agreed?

6 Draw a diagram to illustrate Fermat's fractional approach.

7 Pose for yourself a different gaming problem and try to answer it using the style of reasoning from one of these letters.

8 What fundamental points about probability were established in these letters?

To the last question, I would say primarily that you have to think about all the possible ways in which the game might end and count the proportions in favour of each player.

To do this correctly, you can list the hypothetical, equally likely combinations. Alternatively, by considering the odds at each throw, you can assign a notional 'worth' to each outcome. Pascal did this in whole numbers by choosing a suitably large stake. Fermat did it in fractions. The concepts of possibility space, and of probability as a fraction, both emerge.

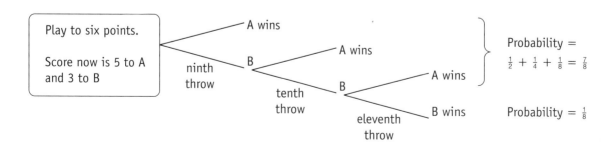

Play to six points.

Score now is 5 to A and 3 to B

ninth throw — A wins

B — tenth throw — A wins

B — eleventh throw — A wins / B wins

Probability $= \frac{1}{2} + \frac{1}{4} + \frac{1}{8} = \frac{7}{8}$

Probability $= \frac{1}{8}$

Sheet 12.4 (top) Mortality tables

One of the early applications of probability was to matters of insurance. The keeping of statistical records was woefully erratic, but in 1693 Edmond Halley was able to present a mortality table to the Royal Society.[3] Later this was used by his friend Abraham de Moivre in a book on probability.

Students should read the first paragraph of the extract and find out the probability of a person their age continuing to be alive for one more year. For instance, of 616 persons aged 17, 610 reached the age of 18, so the probability is $610/616 \approx 0.99$. Compare the probabilities of survival at different ages, according to these statistics.

Sheet 12.4 (bottom) Annuities

The idea of an annuity is that in exchange for a lump sum now, you get a regular income for life, however long or short life may be. De Moivre shows how to work out a fair price to pay for an annual income of £1. First of all, ignoring interest, you could work this out for a person aged 65 (supposing nobody survives beyond 84).

Expected value

$$= \frac{182}{192} + \frac{172}{192} + \frac{162}{192} + \ldots + \frac{23}{192} + \frac{20}{192}$$

$$= \frac{1753}{195}$$

$$\approx 9.14$$

So you should pay £9.14 for the annuity. If you live for more than nine years, you gain. If you live for less, the government (or whoever provides the annuity) will gain. But, as de Moivre says, money bears interest, so to get back £1 after a year at 5% interest, you need only invest $£^1/_{1.05}$ now. To get back £1 after two years, invest $£^1/_{(1.05)^2}$ now. To generalize, you can write r in place of 1.05 and construct the series:

$$\text{Value of £1 annuity} = \frac{B}{Ar} + \frac{C}{Ar^2} + \frac{D}{Ar^3} + \frac{E}{Ar^4} + \ldots$$

Students can do more numerical calculations and/or think about de Moivre's next problem:

> But let us suppose that there should be Expectation of a Sum (which we may call 1) payable once for all whenever it happens that the life ceases within a limited time.

The explanation begins:

> It is plain that the Probability of the Life's ceasing after one year is $(A - B)/A$, and again the Probability of its continuing one year and dropping the next will be $(B/A) \times (B-C)/B$, or barely $(B-C)/A$.

Students can extend this by formulating more problems, for instance:

> Suppose at age 25 you take out insurance to pay £100 if you die within 5 years. What is the expected return according to these statistics?

Answer: Probability of death in the first year is 7/567. Probability of continuing one year, dying the next is:

$$\frac{560}{567} \times \frac{7}{560} = \frac{7}{567}$$

Expected return is:

$$£100 \left(\frac{7}{567} + \frac{7}{567} + \frac{7}{567} + \frac{7}{567} + \frac{8}{567} \right) = £6.35$$

De Moivre suggests a different supposition, 'for instance, that the Party on whose Life this Expectation depends is 10 years of age, and that the Age limited as a Condition of obtaining the sum is 21.' Students could try working this out.[4]

Lettre de M. Pascal à M. de Fermat

Blaise PASCAL (1623–1662)

Pierre de FERMAT (1601–1665)

Mercredi, le 29 Juillet, 1654

Monsieur,

L'impatience me prend aussi-bien qu'à vous!

M. Carcavi brought your letter about the problem of points yesterday evening, and I am tremendously impressed. Although I am still in bed, I can't wait to tell you about an even neater method that I have found. It is such a pleasure to find we think alike — the truth is the same at Toulouse as in Paris.

This is the way I go about it when two gamblers are playing 'the first to three points wins'. Suppose for instance that they have each put 32 pistoles at stake. If the first wins two points and the second one point, and then they decide to cut short the game, how should the 64 pistoles be divided between them?

Consider what might happen on the next throw of the dice. If the first gambler wins the point, the whole 64 belongs to him. If the other one wins, the score is two-two, and so they should take 32 pistoles each. Since they are going to separate without making this throw, the first can argue like this: 'I am sure of 32 pistoles. As for the other 32, perhaps I will have them and perhaps you will have them, the risk is equal. Therefore let us divide the 32 in half.' He will then have 48 pistoles and the other 16.

Now let's suppose that the first has two points and the other none, and they are beginning to play for a point. If the first wins, he will take all of the wager, but if the other wins, behold, they have come back to the previous case of two to one. If they don't wish to play this point, the first should say, 'If I win, I gain 64. If I lose, 48 will legitimately be mine. Therefore give me the 48 and let us divide the other 16 in half.' Thus he will have 56 pistoles and the other 8.

Supposing now the first has only one point and the other none …

I have no time to send you the proof of a difficult point which astonished M. Chevalier de Méré (the one who proposed the question of the dice to me). It made him say haughtily that arithmetic is demented!

…

N.B. These letters are very much abridged, but I have tried to keep to the spirit of the writing.

Lettre de M. Pascal à M. de Fermat

Lundi, le 24 Août, 1654

Monsieur,

I was not able to tell you all my thoughts about the problem of the points in my last letter. I am rather reluctant to do so now in case our harmony, which means so much to me, begins to flag. But I will set out my reasoning for you, and ask you to favour me with your opinion.

When there are only two players, your theory, which depends on combinations, is very just. But let's follow the argument for a three player game in which the first player needs one point to win, the second two, and the third two. You say that it is necessary to see in how many throws the game will certainly be decided. In this case, three more throws will necessarily settle it. Your method is then to see in how many ways three points can be distributed between the three players, count the combinations favourable to each, and divide the stake in that proportion. I could scarcely understand this reasoning if I had not known it already!

It is easy to see your 27 combinations in the table below, where 'a' indicates a throw favourable to the first, 'b' favourable to the second, and 'c' favourable to the third.

a	a	a	a	a	a	a	a	a	b	b	b	b	b	b	b	b	b	c	c	c	c	c	c	c	c	c
a	a	a	b	b	b	c	c	c	a	a	a	b	b	b	c	c	c	a	a	a	b	b	b	c	c	c
a	b	c	a	b	c	a	b	c	a	b	c	a	b	c	a	b	c	a	b	c	a	b	c	a	b	c
1	1	1	1	1	1	1	1	1	1	1	1	1			1			1	1	1	1			1		
				2						2		2	2	2		2						2				
								3									3			3			3	3	3	3

Since the first player lacks one point, all the combinations with one 'a' are favourable to him. There are 19 of these (marked 1). By a similar argument, there are 7 favourable to each of the other two players. If we conclude from this that the stake should be divided in the ratio of 19:7:7 we are making a serious mistake. I hesitate to believe that you would do this, because there are several cases favourable to both the first and the second player, for instance abb. If we allow a half to each player in these cases, which I suppose is what you intend, the division would be in the ratio $16:5\frac{1}{2}:5\frac{1}{2}$.

But if I am not mistaken, this division is unfair. The error arises because we are supposing that they play three throws without exception, whereas in the natural game, play ceases when one player has reached the agreed total. Incidentally, this objection was also raised by M. de Roberval when I showed your work to some of our gentlemen here.

Supposing instead that they play in the natural way, my general method suggests that 17 pistoles should go to the first and 5 pistoles to each of the others.

These, Monsieur, are my reflections on the topic. I shall receive your reply with respect and joy, even if you hold a contrary opinion. Je suis &c.

Pascal

13.3

Lettre de M. de Fermat à M. Pascal

Vendredi, le 25 Septembre, 1654

Monsieur,

Don't worry that our accord is coming to an end. You have strengthened it yourself in thinking to destroy it, and it seems to me that in replying to M. de Roberval for yourself you have also replied for me.

Taking your example of the three gamblers, I find here only 17 combinations favourable to the first and 5 for each of the others; for when you say that the combination acc is good for the first, recollect that everything done after one of the players has won is worth nothing. What does it matter that the third gains two afterwards, since even if he gains thirty it is superfluous? The purpose of this 'fiction' as you have well called it, of extending the game to a certain number of rounds, is only to make the rule easy, and according to my opinion to make all the chances equal; or better, more intelligibly, to reduce all the fractions to the same denominator.

M. de Roberval may perhaps be more satisfied with a solution avoiding this 'fiction', so here it is:

The first player may win in a single round, or in two or in three. He has a one in three chance of winning in a single round, so this possibility is worth $\frac{1}{3}$ of the wager.

If it happens in two rounds, he can gain in two ways — either when the second gambler wins the first and he the second, or when the third gambler wins the first and he the second. But two rounds with three players produce nine chances, so winning in two is worth $\frac{2}{9}$ of the wager.

If he plays three rounds, he can win in only two ways, either the second wins then the third and then himself, or the third, the second and then himself. But three rounds give 27 chances, so the first player has $\frac{2}{27}$ of the chances when they play three rounds.

The sum of the chances which make the first gambler win is thus $\frac{1}{3}$, $\frac{2}{9}$ and $\frac{2}{27}$, which makes $\frac{17}{27}$.

This rule is good and general in all similar cases and makes plain what I said at the outset, that the supposition of a certain number of rounds is no more than a device to reduce various fractions to the same denominator.

At Martinmas I hope to send you an account of my important discoveries concerning numbers. I can be brief since you are a man who understands the whole from half a word. I am sure my method of proof will please you and open the way for many new discoveries.

I am, Monsieur, most heartily your etc.

Fermat

Of Annuities on Lives

BELIEVE IT OR NOT

The SLEEPING GENIUS!
ABRAHAM DE MOIVRE
1667 – 1754
SLEPT 20 OUT OF EVERY 24 HOURS
Yet — HE WAS ONE OF THE GREATEST MATHEMATICIANS IN HISTORY.

Reproduced by kind permission of the *Scottish Sunday Express*.

Suppofe that by help of this Table we would know what the refpective Probabilities are for a Man of 30 to live 1, 2, 3, 4, 5, &c. years. Look for the number 30 in one of the Columns of Age, under which number you will find 31, 32, 33, 34, 35, &c. then over-againft the faid number 30, in the next adjacent Column on the right hand you find 531, under which are written 523, 515, 507, 499, &c. each refpectively correfponding in order to the numbers written in the Column of Age; the meaning of which is, that out of 531 perfons living of the Age of 30, there remain but 523, 515, 507, 499, &c. that attain the refpective Ages of 31, 32, 33, 34, &c. and who confequently do from that Term of 30 live 1, 2, 3, 4, &c. years refpectively.

Dr. Halley's *Table of Obfervations, exhibiting the Probabilities of Life.*

Age	Perfons.	Age	Perf.	Age	Perf.	Age	Perf.	Age	Perf.		Age	Perf.	Age	Perf.	Age	Perf.	Age	Perf.	Age	Perf.
1	1000	8	680	15	628	22	586	29	539		50	346	57	272	64	202	71	131	78	58
2	855	9	670	16	622	23	579	30	531		51	335	58	262	65	192	71	120	79	49
3	798	10	661	17	616	24	573	31	523		52	324	59	252	66	182	73	109	80	41
4	760	11	653	18	610	25	567	32	515		53	313	60	242	67	172	74	98	81	34
5	732	12	646	19	604	26	560	33	507		54	302	61	232	68	162	75	88	82	28
6	710	13	640	20	598	27	553	34	499		55	292	62	222	69	152	76	78	83	23
7	692	14	634	21	592	28	546	35	490		56	282	63	212	70	142	77	68	84	20

Now in order to eftablifh a computation for finding the Value of an Annuity upon a Life of a given Age, let the general quantities A, B, C, D, E, F, &c. reprefent refpectively the perfons living at the Age given, and the fubfequent years.

Now it is very obvious that there being A perfons of the Age given, and one year after B perfons remaining, that the Probability which the person of the given Age has to continue in Life, for one year at leaft, is meafured by the Fraction B/A, and that the Probability which it has to continue in Life for two years at leaft if meafured by the Fraction C/A, and fo on; and that therefore if Money bore no Intereft, it would be fufficient to multiply thofe Probabilities by the Sum to be received Annually, which we fuppofe here to be $= 1$, and the Sum of the Products would exprefs the prefent Value of the Annuity. But as Money bears intereft, let r reprefent the Amount of $1^{L.}$ joined with its Intereft at the year's end, then it is well known that the prefent Values of the Sums to be received Annually would be refpectively $1/r, 1/rr, 1/r^3, 1/r^4$, &c. And therefore multiplying actually thofe Sums by the Probabilities of obtaining them, we fhall have the Value of the Annuity exprefed by a Series.

The apple and the moon

Briefing

Newton demonstrates that gravity, which causes everyday objects to fall to the surface of the earth, is the same force which keeps the moon in its orbit. Whether or not prompted by the fall of an apple, this celebrated intellectual leap repays some detailed study.

The argument is based on proportions, so students of 16+ should be able to follow the gist of it, without prior knowledge of mechanics. The details require a bit of effort and knowledge of basic trigonometry.

For those studying mechanics, it is a wonderful introduction to universal gravitation. Extension possibilities include free fall, equations for uniform circular motion, Kepler's third law and use of a pendulum to determine g.

Isaac Newton (1642–1727).

Background

Early in the year 1665, Isaac NEWTON graduated as a BA of the University of Cambridge. He had already been elected a scholar of Trinity College, which meant staying on to pursue his own research, but these were years of the plague. For fear of infection, the University closed and Newton returned to solitary study at his home on a Lincolnshire farm. Here he developed the calculus, the theory of colours in light, and began to work out a theory of motion, simple yet powerful enough to explain everything from the motion of the planets in space to the tides of the sea, or the outcome of marbles colliding. As an old man, Newton saw this as his golden time for mathematics and science; an extract from his reflections is given on sheet 14.1.

In 1667 he just put the papers away in a drawer and devoted his attention to other things: chemistry (or alchemy?), a reflecting telescope, more mathematics, religion, and so on. Then, in 1684, Edmond Halley visited Cambridge with a question about planetary orbits. This is the same Dr Halley who helped de Moivre (chapter 13) and who amazed his contemporaries by successfully predicting the return of 'his' comet. Newton answered him immediately, could not find his calculations, but promised to write them up and send them on. Over the next few years he was prompted to work with his customary concentration in order to produce a mature and detailed theory of mechanics. Halley persuaded him to publish, under the auspices of the Royal Society, the now famous *Principia* or *Mathematical Principles of Natural Philosophy*. This was in 1687 when Newton was forty-five.

The *Principia* consists of an introduction and three books. In the third book Newton announces: 'I now demonstrate the structure of the System of the World.' He does indeed account for all manner of celestial and terrestrial phenomena in terms of the preceding theory. The same few basic laws are used in each case to work out how things 'ought' to be. Then actual measurements, gleaned from many different observers, are shown to match the predictions. No wonder the impact of this five-hundred page volume was so dramatic, as can be seen in this extract from an ode by Halley:

Lo, for your gaze, the pattern of the skies!
What balance of the mass, what reckonings
Divine! Here ponder too the Laws which God,
Framing the universe, set not aside
But made the fixed foundations of His work.

In the classroom

Introduce as appropriate with Newton's reflections from the top of sheet 14.1.

Read the Principia *extract, bottom of sheet 14.1*
The heading reminds us that, unless we learn Latin, we are forced to read the most renowned English natural philosopher in translation. Notice also the lack of diagrams and formulae. At first reading students will want to know the meaning of 'syzygies' – these are the times of new and full moon when the attraction of sun and

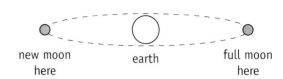

new moon here — earth — full moon here

sun

The moon in the syzygies.

earth act on the moon oppositely or together. Unless you want to deal with the complexity of the actual orbit, it is sensible to take the mean distance at the syzygies and treat the orbit as a circle.

The 'Paris feet' are also intriguing – a standard unit widely used and slightly longer than a British foot.

Do the calculation using Newton's data

Since he gives the results, but not the working-out, this is a suitable task to get students thoroughly involved.

First of all be clear about the problem:

1 We are assuming that the distance of the moon from earth's centre
   = 60 × earth's radius.

2 The time for one revolution of the moon around the earth
   = 27 days 7 hours and 43 minutes
   = 39 343 minutes.

3 The circumference of the earth is 123 249 600 Paris feet, so we can take the radius to be 123 249 600/2π Paris feet.

From these three facts we have to find how far the moon effectively 'falls' towards the earth in one minute. The essential idea here (made explicit in Newton's first law) is that without a force the moon would move off in a straight line rather than curving round in orbit. The simplicity of this concept is difficult to grasp at first. Since we are so used to the moon going round and round, it seems that circling is its natural motion. Newton's genius was to realize that without a force towards the earth, its natural motion would be a straight line off into outer space. A

diagram showing this in a stepwise fashion may help to picture the 'fall'. In reality, of course, the change in direction happens smoothly.

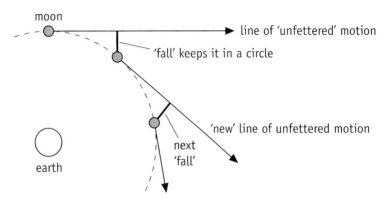

The technical bit of the calculation follows from the same diagram, remembering of course that the 'step' is an artificial concept, but that with small enough steps the error is negligible.

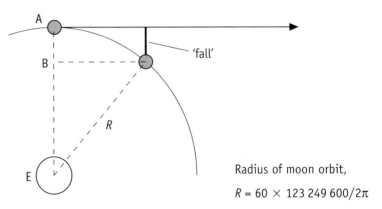

Radius of moon orbit,

$R = 60 \times 123\,249\,600/2\pi$

Working on a time interval of one minute, the angle of rotation must be $360/39\,343°$. The 'fall', $(EA - EB)$, is therefore

$R - R\cos\left(^{360}/_{39\,343}{}^°\right)$

which equals

$R\left\{1 - \cos\left(^{360}/_{39\,343}{}^°\right)\right\}$

A pocket calculator may give zero as the value of $\{1 - \cos(360/39\,343°)\}$, but to 13 decimal places, from a graphic calculator, the value is $1.275\,26 \times 10^{-8}$.

Multiply this by R to find that the moon 'falls' 15.009 feet. Alas, not the same answer as Newton's, so what has happened – nobody seems to know! The difference does not of course invalidate Newton's argument since he already recognizes more than 1 per cent uncertainty in the data. The results match well within experimental error.

The rest of the argument runs smoothly, though there is a hidden assumption, which Newton justified elsewhere, that the earth's gravity acts as from a point at its centre. On this assumption, where we stand at the surface is effectively a distance of one radius from the 'earth'.

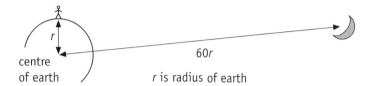

The comparison of the moon with the apple then hinges on the inverse square law, accepted because it fits with Kepler's laws, which in turn are based on direct observation. Sixty times closer to the centre of the earth, the force of gravity should be 60×60 times greater. It is not feasible to observe an object at the earth's surface falling for one minute, but if it were, the distance fallen should be $15 \times 60 \times 60$ feet. Startling confirmation of this came from Huygens' work on the pendulum, which provided a reasonably accurate method of measuring the rate of free fall at the earth's surface.

Since the celestial and the terrestrial measurements match so closely, it is reasonable to conclude that the force which holds the moon in its orbit is the same as the force we normally call gravity.

The 'rules' mentioned in the text are about attitudes to scientific theory. Newton asserts that we should accept the simplest of available explanations. If a physical phenomenon (such as the orbiting of the moon) can be explained in terms of a known effect (such as gravity on earth), then no additional causes should be supposed. This was in conflict with Descartes' hypothesis, popular at that time, that vortices in space caused the motion of heavenly bodies.

Naturally Descartes was highly regarded in France, indeed throughout Europe, but the two world views became a subject of lively debate. Our next chapter recounts how a French translation of the *Principia*, with explanatory notes, made by Émilie du Châtelet, helped towards the eventual acceptance of Newton's ideas.

The moon test

I began to think of gravity extending to ye orb of the moon & ... from Kepler's rule of the periodical times of the Planets ... I deduced that the forces wch keep the Planets in their Orbs must [be] reciprocally as the squares of their distances from the centres about wch they revolve: & thereby compared the force requisite to keep the Moon in her Orb with the force of gravity at the surface of the earth, & found them answer pretty nearly. All this was in the two plague years of 1665–1666. For in those days I was in the prime of my age for invention & minded Mathematicks & Philosophy more than at any time since.

Isaac Newton

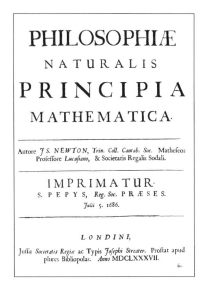

Mathematical Principles of Natural Philosophy
Book III The System of the World

PROPOSITIO IV.   THEOREMA IV.

Lunam gravitare in Terram, & vi gravitatis retrahi semper a motu rectilineo, & in Orbe suo retineri.

That the moon gravitates towards the earth, and by the force of gravity is continually drawn off from rectilinear motion, and retained in its orbit.

The mean distance of the moon from the earth in the syzygies in semi-diameters of the earth, is, according to *Ptolemy* and most astronomers, 59; according to *Vendelin* and *Huygens*, 60; to *Copernicus*, $60\frac{1}{3}$; to Street, $60\frac{2}{5}$; ...

Let us assume the mean distance of 60 diameters in the syzygies; and suppose one revolution of the moon, in respect of the fixed stars, to be completed in 27^{d}. 7^{h}. 43^{m}., as astronomers have determined; and the circumference of the earth to amount to 123 249 600 *Paris* feet, as the *French* have found by mensuration. And now if we imagine the moon, deprived of all motion, to be let go, so as to descend towards the earth with the impulse of all that force by which it is retained in its orb, it will in the space of one minute, describe in its fall $15\frac{1}{12}$ *Paris* feet.

Wherefore, since that force, in approaching to the earth, increases in the proportion of the inverse square of the distance, and, upon that account, at the surface of the earth, is 60·60 times greater than at the moon, a body in our regions, falling with that force, ought in the space of one minute of time, to describe $60·60·15\frac{1}{12}$ Paris feet ... And with this very force we actually find that bodies here upon earth do really descend ...

... And therefore the force by which the moon is retained in its orbit becomes, at the very surface of the earth, equal to the force of gravity which we observe in heavy bodies there. And therefore (by Rule 1 and 2) the force by which the moon is retained in its orbit is that very same force which we commonly call gravity ...

Two women of the Enlightenment

Briefing

Brief biographies provide background for discussion of cultural issues. Extracts from Agnesi's writing offer interesting work on coordinate geometry and the application of differential calculus.

Background

Maria Gaetana AGNESI (1718–1799) and Émilie du CHÂTELET (1706–1749) were the first women in Europe to publish any mathematical works which have survived to the present day. Each was praised for the clarity and exactitude of her work. Their contribution to the advancement of mathematics was significant, in that they expounded important new work of their times. Agnesi in particular brought cohesion to disparate strands, making achievements more readily accessible to the rising generation.

These women were different in character, but both grew up in the early eighteenth century, when attitudes were perceptibly changing. The spread of knowledge, formerly distrusted, began to be considered a positive good and censorship was challenged. Values and habits such as brutality in punishment and entertainment were being questioned. The practice of slavery, however, was barely disputed until the latter half of the century.

This period, widely known as the Enlightenment, was characterized by growing belief in rationality, independence of thought, and, perhaps above all, in Progress. Is it coincidental that some women should emerge in the field of mathematics at such a time?

In the classroom

Sheets 15.1 and 15.2 Biographic outlines[1]
These are intended as a basis for discussion. You could set a task to be carried out in small groups. Students could pick out similarities and differences between du Châtelet and Agnesi in the following spheres: life circumstances, character and work.

This naturally leads into discussion, and possibly further reading and writing. Issues raised might include the role of expositor in times of exploding knowledge and opportunities for women and for other sections of society to engage in mathematics.

Sheet 15.3 The Versiera and other curves
Referring to problem III and the diagram on the sheet, we are:

> given a semicircle, diameter AC, and a line MB normal to the diameter. MB cuts the circle at D and the diameter at B. We have to find a position for M such that AB:BD equals AC:BM.

This condition may seem rather arbitrary until you consider the dotted construction lines. These allow a pictorial interpretation for the ratios: if you complete the rectangle MBCF, then the condition amounts to a requirement that F should lie on the line AD. Triangles ABD and ACF are to be similar. This idea may help to find a few possibilities for M and thus to sketch the locus.

Then follow through the working of the problem. Note that although the point M has, in effect, coordinates (x, y)

'Analifi delle quantità finite , che comunemente chiamafi Algebra Cartefiana,

The beginning of Agnesi's book, published in 1748.

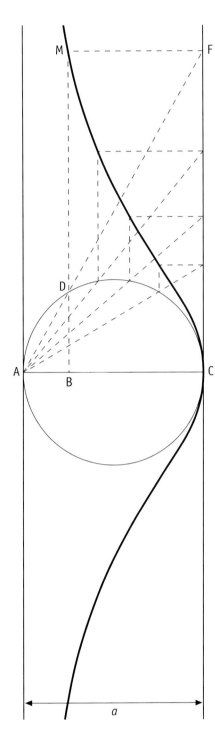

Problem III, the Versiera.

it had not yet become the habit to draw axes. In fact there was flexibility about whether *x* should be across or up the page. I have turned this one around in order to avoid confusion.

The 'property of circles' quoted may not be so well known today. It is simply that the angle in a semicircle is a right angle, so triangle ADC is right-angled at D. DB then divides the triangle into two more mathematically similar triangles, so BD/AB = BC/BD giving:

$$BD^2 = AB.BC = x(a-x).$$

If *x* is less than zero or greater than *a*, the expression for *y* involves the square root of a negative quantity, i.e. *y* is imaginary. The whole locus is confined between the lines $x = 0$ and $x = a$, the former being an asymptote.

An obvious characteristic of the dish-shaped curve is the way it changes from convex in the centre to concave at the fringes. Agnesi used this as an example to demonstrate how differential calculus can be used to determine the point of inflexion where the change takes place. Students can try this: setting the second derivative equal to zero gives the inflexion points $(3a/4, a/\sqrt{3})$ and $(3a/4, -a/\sqrt{3})$.

The cissoid and conchoid were used in ancient Greece in such problems as the doubling of the cube. Now, applying Descartes' method, they can be described by equations:

Cissoid of Diocles. $y = x^2/\sqrt{(ax - x^2)}$, and there is a symmetrical half to this with *y* taking negative values.

Conchoid of Nicomedes. Note that this curve comes in two parts according to whether M is on the same or the opposite side of the line from P:

$$xy = \pm\sqrt{(a^2x^2 - x^4 + 2a^2bx - 2bx^3 + a^2b^2 - b^2x^2)}$$

The curve changes its appearance in an interesting way according to whether $a = b$, $a < b$ or $a > b$. A graph plotter may save some of the labour!

Sheet 15.4 Algebraic notation in 1748

Use this reproduction of the actual text to compare notation then and now. *x* and *y* are used for the variables, *a* for the constant. Note the absence of brackets: a continuous line above the terms serves the same purpose. The $\sqrt{}$ sign is used, as are indices for cube and higher powers, but repetition is used for squares (thus *aa* rather than a^2). This much is in the style of Descartes, but whereas he used ∝ for 'equals', Robert Recorde's = has been adopted here.

Students will have some fun trying to make sense of the question using common sense and the vocabulary given. Then they should solve it by their own method and compare answers!

Émilie du Châtelet

Gabrielle-Émilie (1706–1749), marquise du Châtelet, took Voltaire as her lover, that much is certain. Other details of her life and work are subject to somewhat conflicting accounts, but the story goes something like this.

At Paris in 1706 she was born into a family of good standing, Le Tonnelier de Breteuil. Émilie showed some academic interest and was given an unusually sound education. At eighteen she married a thirty-year-old count. Two children were born, but increasingly her husband was away, concentrating on his military career and Émilie returned to Paris in 1730.

France was prosperous. There were lavish supper parties every evening with card tables for gambling, a pastime that Émilie particularly enjoyed. There was vigorous theatre and café life (arising from the recent introduction of coffee). Men met and talked for hours; ladies could stop their carriages and be served a cup of the modish drink, no doubt taking in all that was going on.

Émile plunged into the life of high society, engaging openly, as was the fashion, in love affairs, but throughout her life she could never relinquish a beau without hurt. She also made friends who would help her with science and mathematical studies. It was to Voltaire, the contentious sceptic and social critic, that she became most devoted and with whom she spent the rest of her life. The story continues according to Voltaire's own memoirs:

> 'I was tired of the lazy and turbulent life led at Paris ... In the year 1733, I met with a young lady who happened to think nearly as I did, and who took a resolution to go with me ... and bury herself in an old ruinous château, upon the borders of Champagne and Lorraine.

> 'We were visited by several of the learned, who came to philosophize in our retreat ... Maupertuis came with John Bernouilli ...
>
> 'We long employed all our attention and powers upon Leibniz and Newton: Madame du Châtelet attached herself first to Leibniz, and explained one part of his system, in a book exceedingly well written, entitled *Institutions de Physique* ... Born with a love of truth, she soon abandoned this system, and applied herself to the discoveries of the great Newton; she translated his whole book on the Principles of Mathematics into French; and when she had afterwards enlarged her knowledge, she added to this book, which so few people understood, an Algebraical Commentary ...'

This work was reprinted in 1966 and remains the only French version of the *Principia*. It undoubtedly contributed to the great progress made by Newtonian ideas during the eighteenth century. Unfortunately Émilie did not live to see its publication. A late pregnancy ended, as so often in those days, with the death of both mother and child in 1749.

Maria Gaetana Agnesi

Maria Gaetana Agnesi (1718–1799) lived in Milan, the first of twenty-one children born to her father, Pietro Agnesi, in the course of three marriages. Both her parents were from wealthy merchant families and their home became noted for its hospitality towards noblemen and scholars.

Pietro fostered the abilities of his children and provided distinguished tutors for the talented Maria Gaetana and her musical sister Maria Teresa. Their mother, Anna Fortunata, died when Maria Gaetana was thirteen years of age. By then the girls were regularly taking part in their father's 'academic evenings'. Maria Gaetana would prepare talks, in Latin of course, on a variety of scientific subjects. She was also an accomplished linguist and would answer questions posed by foreign guests in their own language. Her sister entertained the company by playing her own compositions on the harpsichord.

A new phase of her life began in 1739. A collection of nearly 200 of her talks had been published, but she came to loathe the public display of her talents and wished to enter a convent. This was opposed by her father, but he did allow her to retire from 'society' and devote herself to study and to piety. During the next decade she wrote and supervised the printing of a two-volume book entitled *Institutioni Analitiche* (1748). In this major work, she put into order scattered material from many original authors of the previous century and added extensions of her own.

The result, a systematic treatment of algebra, Cartesian geometry, calculus and differential equations, was highly regarded and praised for its clarity and precision. It was beautifully set out on handmade paper with large type, generous spacing and diagrams on fold-out pages. Agnesi received recognition and gifts from both the Empress of Austria and from the Pope, who also appointed her honorary professor at the University of Bologna.

Amongst many tributes, John Colson, Lucasian professor of mathematics at Cambridge, is reported to have 'found her work to be so excellent that he was at pains of learning the Italian language at an advanced age for the sole purpose of translating her book into English, that the British Youth might have the benefit of it as well as the Youth of Italy'. It seems that by a literal translation of the word 'versiera', he is responsible for a particular dish-shaped curve coming to be known as the 'witch of Agnesi'!

Agnesi, diffident by nature, never lectured at Bologna. After her father's death in 1752, she supervised the education of his younger children and devoted her main effort to charitable work. The last twenty-eight years of her long life were spent in running a large home for elderly women.

15.3

The Versiera of Agnesi and other curves

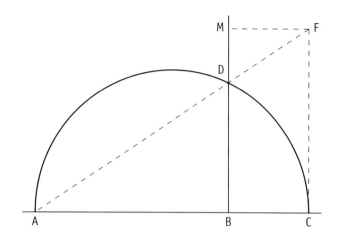

PROBLEMA III.

Given a semicircle, diameter AC, and a line MB normal to the diameter. MB cuts the circle at D and the diameter at B. We have to find a position for M such that AB:BD equals AC:BM.

As B can vary on the diameter, there are infinitely many points M which satisfy this condition; so we look for the equation of the locus.

Let AC = a, AB = x, BM = y.

Then, by the property of circles, BD = $\sqrt{(ax - x^2)}$
and by the condition of the problem, i.e. AB:BD = AC:BM,

$$x:\sqrt{(ax - x^2)} = a:y$$

It follows that

$$y = \frac{a\sqrt{(a-x)}}{\sqrt{x}} \quad \text{or} \quad y^2x = a^2(a - x)$$

and this equation describes the curve called the Versiera.

- Agnesi carried on with this example to discuss asymptotes and imaginary values for y. Can you do the same?

- Taking more examples from her book, you can find the shapes and the equations of these curves; then explore their properties:

PROBLEMA I.   The Cissoid of Diocles

Given a semicircle AEB with centre C. A straight line from A cuts the semicircle at D. M is another point on this line and MP and DO are perpendiculars from M and D onto the diameter. Find the locus of M if CP and CO are to be always equal.

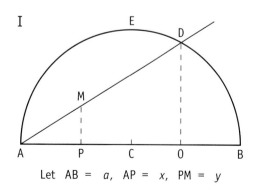

Let AB = a, AP = x, PM = y

PROBLEMA IV.   The Conchoid of Nicomedes

Given a straight line and a fixed point P, distance b from the line. Find the locus of a point M, such that M is at a fixed distance a from the line when measured along MP.

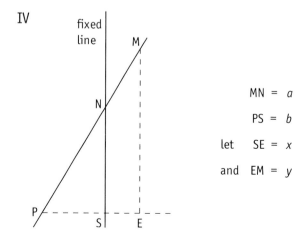

MN = a
PS = b
let SE = x
and EM = y

PROBLEMA II.

237. *Dato l'angolo retto* ABC, (Fig. 134.) *e dato il punto* A *nel lato* AB, *fi cerca il luogo di tutti i punti* M *tali, che condotte per ciafcuno di effi le rette linee* AE, *terminate dal lato* BC *nei punti* E, *fia fempre* EM=EB.

Si tiri una qualunque retta AE, e fia M uno dei punti, che fi cercano; fi abbaffi dal punto M ad AB la perpendicolare MP, e fi chiami $AP = x$, $PM = y$, $AB = a$, farà $PB = a - x$, ed $AM = \sqrt{xx + yy}$, ma per i triangoli fimili APM, ABE, farà x, $y :: a$, BE, dunque $BE = EM = \dfrac{ay}{x}$, ma è anche $AP, PB :: AM, ME$,

cioè $x, a - x :: \sqrt{xx + yy}, \dfrac{ay}{x}$, dunque $ay = \overline{a - x}\sqrt{xx + yy}$,

e quadrando, $ayy = aaxx - 2ax^3 + x^4 + aayy - 2axyy + xxyy$, cioè $\dfrac{aaxx - 2ax^3 + x^4}{2ax - xx} = yy$, e finalmente, effendo la radice di $aaxx - 2ax^3 + x^4$ tanto $ax - xx$, quanto $xx - ax$, farà $y = \dfrac{ax - xx}{\sqrt{2ax - xx}}$, ed $y = \dfrac{xx - ax}{\sqrt{2ax - xx}}$, cioè

$\pm y = \dfrac{ax - xx}{\sqrt{2ax - xx}}$, equazione alla curva, che fi cerca.

Vocabulary

dato	–	given
punto	–	point
nel, nei	–	in
lato	–	side
cerca	–	search, seeking
luogo	–	locus
tali	–	such
che	–	that
condotte per	–	passing through
ciascuno di essi	–	each of them
sempre	–	always

Fig 134

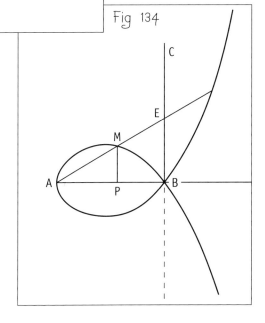

Mental torture

Islamic authors, in the ninth century AD, developed and explained methods of setting up and solving equations by 'doing to one side as you do to the other'. Several mathematicians of the Italian Renaissance struggled to apply these methods to cubic and even quartic equations. The climax of this early effort was the publication of Cardan's *Ars Magna* in 1545.

The famous quarrel with Tartaglia then erupted, but at the same time, stealthily, a new mathematical object emerged! It was the square root of a negative number.

Such an idea would normally be brushed aside as impossible. Any number multiplied by itself gives a positive answer, so that negative numbers cannot have square roots. However, in using the new methods to solve cubic equations, square roots of negatives did sometimes appear, unwelcome, in the calculation.

Cardan obviously experimented with these numbers, dubbed 'sophisticated' or 'imaginary'. Here is an example from his book:

If someone says to you, divide 10 into two parts, one of which multiplied by the other is 30 or 40, it is evident that this is impossible. Nevertheless, we shall solve it in this fashion: We divide 10 into two equal parts, making each 5. These we square, making 25. Subtract 40 if you will, from the 25, leaving a remainder of −15. The root of this added and then subracted from 5 gives the parts, the product of which is 40. These will be $5 + \sqrt{-15}$ and $5 - \sqrt{-15}$.

- Cardan suggested checking this result. Knowing what he is trying to do, you should be able to work out the meaning of his notation shown here.

- Try also to do the calculation yourself, $(5 + \sqrt{-15}) \times (5 - \sqrt{-15})$, by expanding the brackets.

This is what Cardan says about it:

... Putting aside the mental tortures involved, multiply these parts together making 25 − (−15) which is +15, therefore the product is 40.

One of Cardan's contemporaries, Rafael Bombelli, was even more willing to admit these strange quantities into mathematics. He published rules for using them in calculations and showed how they could form apparently genuine solutions to equations.

- You can quite easily follow Bombelli by substituting three different values for x in the equation $x^3 = 15x + 4$:

    firstly $x = 4$

    then $x = 2 + \sqrt{-1}$

    and finally $x = 2 - \sqrt{-1}$

In each case the x^3 on the left-hand side of the equation should reduce to the same value as the right-hand side, proving that the three values are each roots of the equation.

Complex numbers like $2 + \sqrt{-1}$ consist of a real and an imaginary part. They have many applications today, being particularly vital tools in electronics theory. In the seventeenth century they were a curiosity, but their use paved the way for advances in pure mathematics, such as the fundamental theorem of algebra. Loosely this theorem states that a polynomial equation of degree n has exactly n roots if you allow complex numbers. Great minds of the eighteenth century put a lot of effort into proving this theorem.

5 p: R̃ m: 15

5 m: R̃ m: 15

25 m: m: 15 q̄d. eſt 40

Notes and answers

Chapters

Fuller details of references are given in the bibliography.

1 Multiplying in Babylon

1 Fauvel and Gray, pp. 40–2; Time-Life Editors, *The Age of the God-Kings 3000–1500 BC*, p. 20.
2 A photograph of the monument appears in Doblhofer, p. 129, and a drawing in Breasted, p. 184.
3 Van der Waerden, *Science Awakening*, pp. 42–4; Cajori, pp. 8–11.
4 Ibid.
5 Ibid.

2 Doubling in Egypt

1 See Robins and Shute, p. 11, for the plan of the RMP. See Gillings, appendix 6, for the contents of the RMP, chapter 6 for the fraction table, and various chapters for details of the 87 problems.

3 Bamboo in China

1 Li Yan and Du Shiran, p. 4.
2 Ibid., p. 22, quoted from the *Book of Rites*.
3 Ibid., p. 267.
4 Gillespie (ed.).
5 Li Yan and Du Shiran, pp. 13–14.
6 Li Yan and Du Shiran, pp. 48–50; Ronan, p. 39.

4 A taste of Euclid

1 See also chapter 6.
2 BASIC program:
```
10 PRINT 2;3;
20   FOR N = 5 TO 500 STEP 2
30     FOR D = 3 TO SQR(N) STEP 2
40       IF N/D = INT(N/D) THEN 70
50     NEXT D
60     PRINT N;
70   NEXT N
99 END
```
For a computer method based on sieving and further discussion see Engel, p. 61 and chapter 2.
3 Devlin, p. 12.
4 Boyer, pp. 551–2.
5 Heath, *Euclid's Elements*, Book 9, prop. 20; Fauvel and Gray, pp. 127–8.
6 Heath, *Euclid's Elements*, Book 9, prop. 36; Fauvel and Gray, pp. 129–30.

5 Before Pythagoras – and after

1 See, for example, Van der Waerden, *Science Awakening*, p. 76.
2 See, for example, Joseph, pp. 224–39; Thibaut; Seidenberg.
3 For detail see Swetz and Kao.
4 Li Yan and Du Shiran, pp. 30–1.
5 Fauvel and Gray, pp. 32–40; Creighton Buck; Friberg.
6 See, for example, Van der Waerden, *Science Awakening*, p. 76.
7 Heath, *Euclid's Elements*, Book 6, prop. 31.
8 Thibaut, pp. 235–8.

6 Numbering the sand

1 Heath, *The Works of Archimedes*, pp. 221–32; extracts in Fauvel and Gray, pp. 150–2.
2 Menninger, pp. 136–9.
3 Elsewhere in Indian traditions, 'ayuta' and 'niyuta' may have different meanings, e.g. 10^4 and 10^5.
4 Joseph, pp. 250–1.
5 Ibid.
6 Fauvel and Gray, pp. 173–6.
7 Fauvel and Gray, pp. 176–7.
8 Ibid.
9 Heath, *The Works of Archimedes*, pp. 221–32; extracts in Fauvel and Gray, pp. 150–2.
10 *Guardian*, 14 January 1994. You can probably find something more topical.
11 For further detail, see Jain, pp. 23–5.

7 Granaries, dykes and pyramids

1 See chapter 3, 'Background'.
2 See chapter 2, 'Background'.
3 To construct a cube, a wedge, a *yang ma* and a *bie 'nao* from wood, you need a length of timber of square cross-section and a mitre block.

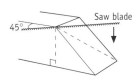

First of all cut off the cube. Next, set the saw at 45° using the mitre block and cut off a wedge. Then, *without sliding the main piece of timber* that remains, rotate it through 90° and cut down using exactly the same mitre setting. The piece cut off will be a *bie 'nao*. The *yang ma* is still attached to the main length of timber; remove it with a normal crosswise cut. If the pieces are to fit together well, allowance may need to be made for the thickness of the saw cut. The problem is diminished by using timber of large cross-section, say 6 cm by 6 cm.

8 Quadrants and artillery

1 Taylor, *The Mathematical Practitioners of Tudor and Stuart England*, p. 17.

9 Arithmetike

1 Howson, p. 7.

2 Gillespie (ed.).

3 See Joseph, pp. 243–9, for a similar Vedic method which extends to 2, 3 and 4 digit numbers.

4 The word 'zenzik' occurs in a contemporary German work by Stifel, but I do not know the origin of the term.

5 See chapter 11.

10 Navigating the oceans

1 See chapter 9, 'Background'.

2 See Taylor, *The Mathematical Practitioners of Tudor and Stuart England*, Biog. 123; Hewson, pp. 162–5.

3 Ore (p. 120) says that Cardan invented this suspension device for the undercarriage of the emperor's vehicle.

4 Mary Rose Trust, *Official Guide* (1989), pp. 16, 35 (Portsmouth PO1 3PX); Hewson, chapter 4.

5 Malin and Stott; Jenkins and Bear.

11 Surveying the land

1 See chapter 9, 'Background'.

2 Taylor, *The Mathematical Practitioners of Tudor and Stuart England*, Biog. 222.

3 Taylor, *The Mathematical Practitioners of Hanoverian England*, pp. 319–20; Owen and Pilbeam chapters 1 and 2.

4 Taylor, *The Mathematical Practitioners of Hanoverian England*, pp. 244–5; Owen and Pilbeam, pp. 7–13; Gillespie (ed.).

12 The *Ladies' Diary*

1 Capp, p. 239.

2 *Edinburgh Review*, 1808, vol. 11, pp. 282–3.

3 Somerville, pp. 46–7, 53–4, 79.

4 Jewish and Christian scriptures, Genesis 9.13.

5 Further detail in Cranfield and/or Black.

6 $\frac{1}{3}\pi h(a^2+ab+b^2)$ where a and b are the radii of the upper and lower circular faces and h is the distance between them. See Vogel or Li Yan and Du Shiran.

13 Calculating with chance

1 Discussed fully in Hacking.

2 David, p. 37.

3 'An estimate of the degrees of mortality of mankind, drawn from curious tables of the births and funerals at the city of Breslau …', *Phil. Trans.*, 1693.

4 Expectation on £1 is £$\frac{69}{661}$ = £0.1044.

15 Two women of the Enlightenment

1 Biographical information from Gillespie (ed.), and Grinstein and Campbell and other sources given in these volumes.

Sheets

1.2 Adapted from an ancient text about the training of scribes, quoted in A. J. Sjoberg, 'In praise of the scribal art', *Journal of Cuneiform Studies*, **24** (1971/2), 127.

2.1 Gillings, pp. 5, 9, for hieroglyphic symbols. Quotation from Papyrus Lansing, Robins and Shute, p. 4.

Answers: 1. 84 jugs 2. 84 loaves 3. 23 100 bricks 4. 6000 square cubits (though more likely this would have been done as $\overline{2}$ khet by $1\overline{5}$ khet with the answer $\overline{2}$ $\overline{10}$ setat). (1 khet = 100 cubits, 1 setat = 1 square khet) 5. 720 ro 6. 432 loaves, 666 jugs 7. 14 cows 8. 16 $\overline{2}$ palms length 9. Divide by 34 to give 4 each leaving 8 for the boatman 10. Divide by 30 to find one portion is 8 $\overline{5}$, which is the amount due to scribe and guard, director gets 82, priest 41, worker 4 $\overline{10}$ 11. 28 $1\overline{3}$ hekat (Egyptian year was 12 months of 30 days plus 5 days to celebrate major gods from their large pantheon)

2.2 Robins and Shute, p. 12, for hieratic numerals; Gillings, appendix 2, for variations. Van der Waerden, *Science Awakening*, plate 3 and caption, and Gillings, chapter 9, for leather roll.

3.1 Li Yan and Du Shiran, p. 15, for Han strip; p. 267 for tones of voice.

5.2 Swetz and Kao, pp. 14–16.

5.3 Swetz and Kao, chapter 2. 10 Chinese inches = 1 Chinese foot.

Triplets involved: 7, 24, 25;
20, 21, 29;
60, 91, 109;
5, 12, 13.

5.4 Proclus, pp. 337–8. Aubrey in Dick, pp. 227, 230.

7.1 The problems are numbered according to the source, chapters 1 and 5 of the *Nine Chapters of the Mathematical Art*. They are based on a translation made by F.R. Watson from Vogel. In the construction questions, 3 units of length are used which Vogel calls Klafter, Fuss and Zoll. I have converted all to the basic Fuss or foot (1 Klafter = 10 Fuss, 1 Fuss = 10 Zoll). Remember that in the Chinese text all the answers are stated. I have left them as questions except for examples 1 and 2 which establish the units of area.

Answers: 1. 1 Mu = 240 square paces 2. 1 Bu = 1 square pace 25. 126 Bu 26. 23.$\frac{5}{6}$ Bu or 23.83 Bu 27. 9 Mu 144 Bu or 2304 Bu 28. 23 Mu 70 Bu or 5590 Bu 29. 1 Mu 135 Bu or 375 Bù 30. 46 Mu 232$\frac{1}{2}$ Bu or 11 272$\frac{1}{2}$ Bu

7.2 *Answers:* 2. 1 897 500 cubic feet 3. 6774 cubic feet 4. 7112 cubic feet; 16$\frac{2}{111}$ men (as given!) 5. 4375 cubic feet; 7$\frac{427}{3064}$ men (as given!) 6. 10 943.8 cubic feet approx.; 232$\frac{4}{15}$ cubic feet or 232.3 cubic feet 7. 10 074 586 cubic feet approx.; 33 582 men

7.3 Gillings, pp. 187–93, for Moscow papyrus method.

7.4 Van der Waerden, *Geometry and Algebra in Ancient Civilizations*, pp. 40–4 for Liu Hui.

7.5 Gillings, pp. 139–53, for discussion of Egyptian method. Li Yan and Du Shiran, pp. 44, 41, for Chinese methods.

8.2 *Answers:* 1. 45° 2. 60° or 30° 3. 50° or 40° 4. 15° 5. 22½° 6. 35° 7. 35° 8. 9½°

8.3 Extracts from Belli and Babington.

8.4 *Answer: 2* The castle is 274.7 yards distant from B.

9.4 From Recorde's *Whetstone of Witte*. (All other sheets from editions of *The Ground of Arts*.) (The '*Cubike numbers*' make sense if read as '2 times (2 twice)', etc.)

10.1 Quotations from 1702 edition, Chapter VII and Chapter VIII.

Answers: 1. 3 miles an hour W 2. 1 mile an hour W (i.e. backwards) 3. 6 miles an hour E.

10.2 Quotations from 1702 edition.

Answers: 4. $6\frac{32}{100}$ miles hourly, South 18 deg. 26 min. Easterly 5. West 13 deg. 57 min Southerly, 747 miles 12. $\tan^{-1}$ (57.4/138.6) West of North, or a bearing of $360° - 22.5° = 337.5°$. North by West means a direction 11.25° to the West of North, i.e. a bearing of 348.75°. 8. (Modified question) Bearing 248°, 6.4 min.

11.1 to 11.3 Quotations from W. Leybourn, *Cursus Mathematicus*, 1690.

11.4 to 11.6 From Mudge and Dalby.

12.1 *Answers:*

1712 22 years 8 months 1713 27 years
1917 Rover is now 10 years old. (This problem is adapted from item 47 in Dudeney's *Amusements in Mathematics*, first published in 1917 and running to many reprints.)
1935 If a, b and c are the children's ages, we deduce from the conversation that $(a+b+c)^2$ gives the same result as $a+b^2+c^3$, and since the children are all at school, we are presumably looking for values between 5 and 19. In 1935, intelligent trial and error was probably the best method. Only one solution was offered in this range: Alice 13, Brian 16, and Clare 11. Today, the difficulty of solving such a problem is transformed by the possibility of using a computer. Pupils can easily surpass the 1935 puzzlers and find several alternative solutions with this simple BASIC program:

```
10   FOR A = 5 TO 19
20     FOR B = 5 TO 19
30       FOR C = 5 TO 19
40         IF (A+B+C)^2 = A + B*B + C*C*C
THEN PRINT A,B,C
50         NEXT C
60       NEXT B
70   NEXT A
```

(This problem is adapted from problem 33 in H. Phillips (Caliban), *The Sphinx Problem Book*, Faber and Faber.)

12.2 *Answers to Mrs Sidway's questions*

The depth of the kettle would have to be increased by 6.38 inches. By trial, or by calculus, the cylinder should be cut at $\frac{1}{3}$ the height of the cone.

12.3 *Answer to question from 1709*

If this pendulum has length n inches and makes n vibrations in one minute, the time of one vibration is $60/n$ seconds. By 'vibration' is meant half of a complete oscillation, the 'tick' and 'tock' of a clock each counting as one vibration or beat. Since the square of the time period is in proportion to the length (time for a complete oscillation $= 2\pi\sqrt{(l/g)}$ means that t^2 varies as length, l):
the ratio $(60/n)^2$ to l is equal to n to 39.2
$$n^3 = 60^2 \times 39.2$$
$$n = 52.0630$$
A pendulum of length 52.1 inches vibrates 52.1 times per minute. You could try a similar calculation for centimetres, given the modern value that a 0.994 metre pendulum has a 1 second beat. Then maybe find the length of the half-second pendulum, which was frequently used in clocks.

Answers:
A 71 centimetre pendulum vibrates 71 times per minute.
A 24.85 centimetre pendulum has a half-second beat.

Answers to questions from 1713
With the suppositions suggested, the heavy body falls in 48 seconds, and sound rises to the same height in 34 seconds. To make the times equal, the height would have to be nearer to 14 miles or 22.4km. The body would strike the ground at a speed of 1480 mph or 662 metres/second!

13.1, 13.2, 13.3 Letters abridged from translations given in David, Appendix 4, and Smith (Source Book), both based on P. Tannery and C. Henry, *Œuvres de Fermat*, vol. 2 (Gauthier-Villars 1894).

13.4 Quoted from de Moivre, pp. 211–12, 253.

14.1 Quotations from Westfall, p. 143; and Newton, pp. 407–8.

Folios

Folio 1 Chinese magic squares

For magic squares see a post-1938 edition of Rouse Ball. Needham, vol. 3, pp. 55–61, for squares; vol. 2, pp. 261–72 for mystical connotations; see also Ronan, pp. 18–24.

4-spoke wheel: 5 in centre, pairs 1,9; 8,2; 7,3; 4,6 on spokes, totals 20 round circles. Will also work with 1 or 9 in the centre, pairs adding to 11 or 9, with 22 or 18 round the circles.

8-spoke wheel: 1 in centre, pairs adding to 19; 9 in centre, pairs adding to 18; 17 in centre, pairs adding to 17 on spokes.

Folio 3 Fingers for number symbols

Fold the 4th and 5th fingers of the left hand into the palm to represent 8. Then stretch out the 5th finger, which represents 7 (i.e. take away 7). You are left with just the 4th finger folded down and this represents 6.

Folio 5 Mental torture

Quotations composed from Smith (Source Book) and Cardan tr. Witmer, p. 219. There is disagreement about the translation of 'mental torture'.

Bibliography

General reference books

C.B. Boyer, *A History of Mathematics* (Wiley 1968)

F. Cajori, *A History of Mathematical Notations*, vol. 1 (Open Court 1974, original edn 1928)

J. Fauvel, *Mathematics through History: A Resource Guide* (QED Books 1990)

J. Fauvel and J. Gray (eds), *The History of Mathematics: A Reader* (Macmillan with The Open University 1987)

C.C. Gillespie (ed.), *Dictionary of Scientific Biography*, 16 vols (Scribners 1970–80)

D.E. Smith, *History of Mathematics*, 2 vols (Dover 1951, original edn 1923)

Select bibliography for part 1

A.L. Basham, *The Wonder That Was India* (Sidgwick and Jackson 1954)

J.H. Breasted, *Ancient Times* (Ginn 1916)

C. Blunden and M. Elvin, *Cultural Atlas of China* (Phaidon/Oxford 1983)

E. Chiera, *They Wrote in Clay* (Chicago 1956)

R. Creighton Buck, 'Sherlock Holmes in Babylon', *American Mathematical Monthly*, **87** (1980), 338–45

K. Devlin, *Mathematics: The New Golden Age* (Penguin 1988)

E. Doblhofer, *Voices in Stone* (Souvenir Press 1961)

A. Engel, *Elementary Mathematics from an Algorithmic Standpoint*, tr. F.R. Watson (Keele Mathematical Education Publications 1984).

J. Friberg, 'Methods and traditions of Babylonian mathematics', *Historia Mathematica*, **8** (1981), 277–318

A. Gardiner, *Egypt of the Pharaohs* (Oxford University Press 1964)

R.J. Gillings, *Mathematics in the Time of the Pharaohs* (Dover 1982, original edn 1972)

T.L. Heath, *The Thirteen Books of Euclid's Elements, translated from the text of Heiberg*, 3 vols (Dover 1956, original edn 1908)

T.L. Heath, *The Works of Archimedes* (Original edn Cambridge University Press 1897 and Supplement 1912)

L.C. Jain, *Exact Sciences from Jaina Sources*, vol. 2 (Rajastha-Jaipur 1982)

G.G. Joseph, *The Crest of the Peacock: Non-European Roots of Mathematics* (I.B. Tauris 1991)

M. Loewe, *Everyday Life in Early Imperial China* (Batsford 1968)

K. Menninger, *Number Words and Number Symbols*, tr. P. Broneer (MIT Press 1969)

H. Midonick, *The Treasury of Mathematics*, vol. 1 (Penguin 1965)

J. Needham, *Science and Civilization in China*, vols 2, 3 and 4 (Cambridge University Press 1959)

O. Neugebauer, *The Exact Sciences of Antiquity* (Harper 1962, original edn 1952)

Proclus, *A Commentary on the First Book of Euclid's Elements*, tr. G.R. Morrow (Princeton University Press 1970)

G. Robins and C. Shute, *The Rhind Mathematical Papyrus* (British Museum Publications 1987)

W. Rodzinskii, *A History of China*, vol. 1 (Pergamon 1979)

C.A. Ronan, *The Shorter Science and Civilization in China*, vol. 2 (Cambridge University Press 1981, an abridgement of Needham)

W.W. Rouse Ball, *Mathematical Recreations and Essays* (Macmillan 1947, original edn 1892, revised H.M.S. Coxeter 1938)

A. Seidenberg, 'The origin of mathematics', *Archive for the History of Exact Sciences*, **18** (1978), 301–42

F.J. Swetz and T.I. Kao, *Was Pythagoras Chinese?* (Pennsylvania State University Press 1977)

G. Thibaut, 'On the Sulvasutras', *Journal of the Asiatic Society of Bengal*, **44** (1875), 227–75

Time-Life Editors, *The Age of the God-Kings 3000–1500 BC* (Time-Life Books 1987)

B.L. van der Waerden, *Geometry and Algebra in Ancient Civilizations* (Springer-Verlag 1983)

B.L. van der Waerden, *Science Awakening* (Noordhoff 1954)

K. Vogel, *Neun Bücher arithmetischer Technik* (Vieweg & Sohn 1968)

F. Watson, *India, A Concise History* (Thames and Hudson 1992, original edn 1974)

Li Yan and Du Shiran, *Chinese Mathematics: A Concise History*, tr. J.N. Crossley and A.W.-C. Lun (Clarendon Press 1987)

Yong Yap and A. Cotterell, *The Early Civilization of China* (Weidenfeld and Nicholson 1975)

Select bibliography for part 2

TK indicates reference to the edition in the Charles W. Turner Collection at Keele University, Staffordshire.

M.G. Agnesi, *Institutione Analitiche*, 2 vols (Milan 1748) **TK**

J. Babington, *A Short Treatise of Geometrie* (Thomas Harper 1635; reproduction Da Capo Press 1971)

S. Belli, *Libro del misurar con la vista …* (Venetia, per Domenica de' Nicolini 1565) **TK**

J. Black, *The English Press in the Eighteenth Century* (Croom Helm 1987)

R. Bombelli, *L'Algebra* (Bologna, per Giovanni Rossi 1579) **TK**, tr. F.R. Smith (Feltrinelli 1966)

B. Capp, *English Almanacs 1500–1800* (Cornell University Press 1979)

G. Cardano, *Ars Magna* (1545). *De Subtilitate* (1559) and *Practica Arithmetica* (1539) **TK**

G. Cardano, *The Great Art or The Rules of Algebra*, tr. T.R. Witmer (MIT Press 1968)

G. Cardano, *The Book of My Life*, tr. J. Stoner (Dent 1931) **TK**

G.A. Cranfield, *The Development of the Provincial Newspaper 1700–1760* (Oxford University Press 1962)

F.N. David, *Games, Gods and Gambling* (Griffin 1962)

O.L. Dick, *Aubrey's Brief Lives* (Penguin 1987, original edn 1949)

R.G. Doty, *Money of the World* (Ridge Press 1978)

J. Fauvel *et al.* (eds), *Let Newton Be* (Oxford University Press 1988)

L.S. Grinstein and P.J. Campbell, *Women of Mathematics: A Biobibliographic Sourcebook* (Greenwood Press 1987)

I. Hacking, *The Emergence of Probability* (Cambridge University Press 1984)

A.R. Hall, *Ballistics in the Seventeenth Century* (Cambridge University Press 1952)

J.B. Hewson, *A History of the Practice of Navigation* (Brown, Son and Ferguson, second edn 1983)

A.G. Howson, *A History of Mathematics Education in England* (Cambridge University Press 1982)

G. Jenkins and M. Bear, *The Tarquin Globe* (Tarquin, Norfolk 1986, available from Norfolk IP21 5JP)

W. Leybourn, *Cursus Mathematicus*, Mathematical Sciences in Nine Books (Thomas Basset, London 1690) **TK**

S. Malin and C. Stott, *The Greenwich Meridian* (Ordnance Survey, Southampton 1984, available from Southampton SO9 4DH)

A. Maurel, *The Romance of Mme du Châtelet & Voltaire*, tr. W. Mostyn (Hutchinson) **TK**

A. de Moivre, *The Doctrine of Chances* (second edn London 1738) **TK**

W. Mudge and I. Dalby, *An Account of the Operations Carried on for Accomplishing a Trigonometrical Survey of England and Wales*, vol. 1 (London 1799) **TK**

I. Newton, *The Mathematical Principles of Natural Philosophy*, tr. A. Motte 1729, revised F. Cajori (University of California Press 1962)

R. Norwood, *The Seaman's Practice* (London 1702, first edn 1637) **TK**

O. Ore, *Cardano, the Gambling Scholar* (Princeton University Press 1953)

T. Owen and E. Pilbeam, *Ordnance Survey, Map Makers to Britain since 1791* (Ordnance Survey and HMSO 1992)

J. Porteous, *Coins in History* (Weidenfeld and Nicolson 1969)

R. Recorde, *The Ground of Arts* (1543 edition, reproduction Da Capo Press 1969, 1575 and 1615 editions) **TK**

R. Recorde, *The Whetstone of Witte* (London 1557) **TK**

D.E. Smith, *A Source Book in Mathematics* (Dover 1959, original edn McGraw Hill 1929)

Martha Somerville, *Personal Recollections of Mary Somerville (by her daughter)* (John Murray 1873)

N. Tartaglia, *Quesiti, et Inventioni Diverse …* (Venetia 1546) **TK**

E.G.R. Taylor, *The Mathematical Practitioners of Tudor and Stuart England* (Cambridge University Press 1954)

E.G.R. Taylor, *The Mathematical Practitioners of Hanoverian England* (Cambridge University Press 1966)

R.S. Westfall, *Never at Rest: A Biography of Isaac Newton* (Cambridge University Press 1980)

Curriculum index

Numbers indicate which photocopiable sheets are relevant to the mathematical topics listed. Guidance on using the sheets is given in the text. Where topics are discussed in a chapter but without photocopy material, this is indicated by 't'.

Number and measuring units

Reading scale divisions	8.1	8.2				
Adding whole numbers	F2	9.1				
Multiplication facts	1.1	3.1	9.3			
Problems using multiplication and division (several digits):						
with whole numbers	2.1	7.1	7.2	7.3		
when it won't divide exactly	1t	2.1	1.2b (hard)			
Measuring units and money	2.1	9.2	9.5	10.1		
with conversion	1t	9.2				
Place value in whole numbers	1.1	1.2a	2.1	3.1	F3	9.1
Place value in fractions	9.5	1.2b (hard)				
Using equivalent fractions, adding	2.2					
Reading and using large numbers	6t					
Comparison by percentage	9.2					
percentage error in measurement	11.6	11.7				
Ratios and proportion	2.1	8.2	8.3	10.1		
with scale drawing	11.1	11.2	11.5			
Squares and square roots	5.1	5.2	5.3			
higher powers	9.4					
Properties of odd, even and prime numbers	4t					
Complex numbers	F5 (advanced)					

Algebra

Simple pattern in number	1.1	3.1		
Doubling and halving strategies	2.1			
Division as inverse of multiplication	2.1	1.2b (hard)		
Using a procedure expressed in words	7.1	7.2	7.3	11.2
expressed in symbols	7.5	7.4		
Expressing a procedure symbolically	7.3	7.5	9.3t	
Generating and reasoning with prime numbers	4t			
Expressing general rules for odds and evens	4t			
Harder number patterns and progressions	3t	4t	9.1	
Introduction to indices, relation of powers and roots	9.4			
Meaning of reciprocals	1.2b			
Manipulating algebraic expressions	F4	15.3 (advanced)	15.4 (advanced)	
Constructing and solving equations (with fractions)	12.1			
Complex roots of quadratic and cubic equations	F5 (advanced)			

Geometry and mensuration

Measuring and drawing angles	8.1	11.1	11.2	
Compass points and bearings	10.1			
Angle sum of polygon	11.2			
Constructing figures in 2D	5.1	7.1	11.1	11.2
3D constructions	7.4			
Problems involving areas	7.1	5.2	5.4	
Volumes by counting cubes	6t			
Volumes of prisms and pyramids	7.2	7.3	7.4	
Volume of cylinder and perimeter–area relation for circle	7.5			
Volume of cone frustum and optimum cylinder	12.2			
Area of circle and circle sector	7.5			
Pythagoras theorem	5 (text and all sheets)			
Mathematical similarity	5.4	8.2	8.3	
Tangent ratio in right-angled triangle	8.2	8.4		
Vector addition in context	10.2			
Congruent triangles	8.4			
Use of sine (and cosine) rule	(10.2)	11.1	11.6	11.7
Locus and equation of curves	15.3 (advanced)		15.4 (advanced)	

Data handling and probability

Choosing appropriate average and recognizing range	11.1	11.2	
Planning observation sheet for recording data	11.2		
Probabilities of combined events	F1	13.3 (advanced)	13.4 (advanced)
Listing outcomes	13t	13.1 (advanced)	13.2 (advanced)
Probability from statistical data	13.4 (advanced)		

Uses and applications of mathematics

These are emphasized throughout, but note in particular:

Practical activity	1t	3t	6t	7.4	
	8.1	8.2	11.1	11.2	11.3
Investigating and reasoning	1.1	1.2	2.2	3.1	4t
	5t	6t	7.3	7.4	8.4
	9.1	9.3	9.5	11.6	11.7
	12.1	13.1	13.2	13.3	14.1
Accuracy and approximations	6t	7.5	8.1	8.4	
	10.1	11.1	11.2	11.6	11.7
Probability and statistics in an actuarial context	13.4 (advanced)				
Universal gravitation, free fall and pendulum	12.3 (advanced)		14.1 (advanced)		

Index